GARCIA V. VERTEX MANUFACTURING COMPANY

SECOND EDITION
Formerly titled Garcia v. Pinnacle

Garcia v. Vertex Manufacturing Company

Second Edition
Formerly titled Garcia v. Pinnacle

William S. Bailey
Fury Bailey
710 – 10th Avenue East
P.O. Box 20397
Seattle, WA 98102
(206) 726-6600
bill@furybailey.com

Frederick C. Moss
Southern Methodist University
Dedman School of Law
Dallas, Texas 75275-0116
fmoss@smu.edu

NATIONAL INSTITUTE FOR TRIAL ADVOCACY

Address inquiries to:

Reprint Permission
National Institute for Trial Advocacy
1685 38th Street, Suite 200
Boulder, CO 80301-2735
Phone: (800) 225-6482
Fax: (720) 890-7069
E-mail: permissions@nita.org

ISBN 978-1-60156-107-7

FBA 1107

13 12 11 10   10 9 8 7 6 5 4 3 2 1

Printed in the United States of America

 Wolters Kluwer

Official co-publisher of NITA.
WKLegaledu.com/NITA

ACKNOWLEDGMENTS

The authors would like to thank and acknowledge Dr. Linda M. Ojemann of the University of Washington Medical Center, an outstanding neurologist and clinician specializing in the diagnosis and treatment of seizure disorders, for her assistance with the medical information contained in this case file. The authors also would like to express their appreciation to vocational rehabilitation and life-care plan expert Mr. John Fountaine, M.A., CRC of OSC Vocational Systems, Bothell, Washington, for his knowledgeable assistance with the potential medical and treatment costs presented in this case file.

CONTENTS

INTRODUCTION

This is a personal injury case involving the tip-over of an extended reach personnel lift, brought by a shipyard worker who fell seventy feet while using the lift on the job. The lift was owned by his employer, Marine Resources Shipyard (MRS), which bought the lift from its manufacturer, defendant Vertex Manufacturing, some three months earlier.

Plaintiff seeks to recover damages from the defendant manufacturer on the basis that it negligently failed to design a reasonably safe personnel lift. Defendant denies any negligence on its part.

The plaintiff's employer, MRS, hired an engineering consultant to investigate this accident shortly after its occurrence. This engineer determined that both of the lift's anti-tip-over mechanisms ("Load Management System") were not functioning when the tip-over occurred, and, therefore, failed to warn the plaintiff of the imminence of the tip-over and to protect him from it. This expert further found that the circuit boards that operated the Load Management System's anti-tip-over mechanisms had simultaneously shorted out for an unknown reason because they were faultily designed. Moreover, the expert found that the defendant failed to design the lift so that it would warn workers using the lift that the anti-tip-over safety systems were not functioning. The expert will testify that the lift was negligently designed and, as such, was not reasonably safe. Moreover, plaintiff charges that there were post-manufacture safety changes in the design of the circuit cards on the anti-tip-over system that customers, including MRS, were never told about.

The manufacturer denies this, saying that the changes were made simply for "customer convenience" and that there was no need to send out a service bulletin on this design change to those who owned the existing machines.

The safety and reliability manager of the manufacturer will testify that their product is very reliable, meeting or exceeding all industry standards. However, he must concede that there was a similar tip-over accident five years earlier.

Defendant further alleges that plaintiff's employer was at fault in failing to properly train workers to use personnel lifts on the job. Despite a prominent decal on the ground control station of the lift that states the anti-tip-over load management system is to be tested prior to use of the lift each day, none of the MRS workers, including plaintiff, did so on the day of the accident.

There is a significant dispute on plaintiff's prayer for damages. Plaintiff claims that he sustained a closed head injury, which impairs his ability to engage in the normal activities of everyday life. Plaintiff further alleges that the closed head injury is associated with both a seizure disorder and a personality change. Plaintiff states that he now is a recluse, fearful, with poor impulse control. All of these claims are hotly disputed by defendant. However, the bilateral ankle fractures he suffered in the fall are not controverted. They were surgically repaired successfully. After rehabilitation, he regained reasonable mobility.

The laws of the State of Nita govern the trial of this case. There is no issue of jurisdiction, venue, service of process, propriety of the parties, or question that the defendant was in the scope and course of employment at the time of his injury. The applicable laws are contained in the required stipulations and in the proposed jury instructions set forth at the end of the case file.

INSTRUCTIONS AND STIPULATIONS FOR USE AS A FULL TRIAL

When this case is used for a full trial on both liability and damages, the parties are limited to calling the following witnesses:

For the Plaintiff:

> Raymond Garcia
> John Machado
> Werner Gerhard
> Stella Garcia
> Dr. Elena Moretti

For the Defendant:

> Marvin Felix
> Melvin Demsky
> Dr. J. Marlene Coffin

If the case is tried on liability only, Stella Garcia and Drs. Moretti and Coffin are not necessary and should not be called as witnesses. All of the witnesses, including the plaintiff, can be of either gender. For example, if the plaintiff is a female, it should be assumed that all references to "Raymond Garcia" in the case file read "Rita Garcia." Likewise, John Machado could be June Machado, and Stella Garcia could be Raymond's father, Stanley Garcia.

When dates are given, years are expressed as "YR-[X]." This means the current year (YR) *minus* the given number of years (-X). Thus, if this case were to be tried in 2011, and a document is dated "YR-2", then counsel and witnesses should refer to the date as "2009" (2011 minus 2 years = 2009), not "Year minus 2" or "Year 2."

Required Stipulations

1. The laws of the State of Nita govern the trial of this case. The State of Nita Rules of Civil Procedure allow a defendant who is sued for negligence to allege contributory negligence of another person or entity without having to implead that person or entity as a party to the lawsuit. The applicable law is contained in the proposed jury instructions set forth at the end of the case file. The defense may not raise an issue regarding jurisdiction, venue, service of process, or propriety of the parties.

2. The Nita Rules of Evidence and Procedure apply and are identical to the Federal Rules of Evidence and Rules of Procedure, except cross-examination is not limited to the scope of direct examination and credibility as under the FRE.

3. The statements of the witnesses in their summarized depositions are admissible to the same extent as testimony in a full and complete deposition transcript. Everything said in a witness's statement, therefore, should be treated as a response to a question at deposition.

4. Each witness must admit the authenticity of the signature on his or her deposition summary and that he or she reviewed the testimony before signing it.

5. The date of the fall of the Vertex lift that injured Garcia was October 2, YR-2, and this was a weekday.

6. The trial court held a pretrial hearing on both parties' challenges to all of the other side's expert witnesses' qualifications and the admissibility of their opinions under Nita's Rules of Evidence and the Nita Supreme Court case that adopted the U.S. Supreme Court's decision in *Daubert v. Merrell Dow Pharmaceuticals, Inc.*, 509 U.S. 579 (1993). The trial court has ruled that all of the parties' listed experts (including Marvin Felix) are qualified and their opinions are admissible.

7. Both parties have stipulated that the three computer-generated graphics of the lift's fall (Exhibits 20a, b, c) were prepared by an expert accident reconstruction firm hired by the plaintiff and that the three graphics are admissible at trial.

8. The defendant filed a motion in limine asking the court to exclude from evidence under Nita Evidence Rule 407, Subsequent Remedial Measures, the change it made to the load management system's circuit boards after it sold to Marine Resources the Vertex 110 Personnel Lift that fell and injured plaintiff. The trial judge has overruled the defendant's motion and ruled that the change in design is admissible.

9. On motion by the plaintiff, the trial court has taken judicial notice that the book, *Diagnosing Closed Head Injuries* by Wilbert Von Bulow, PhD, an excerpt of which is in this file, is a "learned treatise" under Nita Evidence Rule 803(18) and that the excerpts in this file are authentic.

10. The parties have stipulated that the actual "out-of-pocket" medical expenses that Raymond Garcia has incurred as a result of the accident under litigation here, up to the date of the trial, total $25,000. The parties further have stipulated that Raymond Garcia lost three months of wages as a result of the accident, totaling $7,500.

11. The jury is not to be asked to assess damages for physical and emotional pain and suffering.

In the Circuit Court of
Darrow County, Nita
Civil Division

RAYMOND GARCIA,	)	
	)	Civil Action
Plaintiff,	)	CA 1948-IL
	)	
v.	)	Complaint
	)	
VERTEX MANUFACTURING COMPANY	)	
	)	
Defendant.	)	
	)	

Raymond Garcia, for his cause of action against defendant, Vertex Manufacturing Company ("Vertex"), states and alleges as follows:

I. Parties

1.1   At all times material, plaintiff Raymond Garcia, resided and was employed in Darrow County, Nita.

1.2   At all times material, defendant Vertex was a business corporation located in Nita City, Darrow County, Nita, and was involved in manufacturing personnel lift equipment.

1.3   On or about June 25, YR-2, Marine Resources Shipyard ("Marine Resources") purchased a Vertex 110 Personnel Lift from the defendant for use in Marine Resources' Nita City shipyard.

II. Liability

2.1   On or about October 2, YR-2, plaintiff was an employee of Marine Resources, performing his job while in the basket of the Vertex 110 Personnel Lift device referred to in paragraph 1.3. The lifting device fell over, causing plaintiff and the basket to fall to the ground below. The negligence of the above-named defendant was a direct and proximate cause of the accident and caused plaintiff Raymond Garcia to sustain serious personal injuries.

2.2   The negligence of the defendant, which proximately caused plaintiff Raymond Garcia's injuries, includes, but is not limited to:

a.   Defendant's design of the Vertex 110 Personnel Lift was not reasonably safe for its normal and expected uses; and

b.   Vertex negligently failed to issue to Marine Resources adequate warnings or instructions regarding the possible failure of the lift's anti-tip-over safety systems ("Load Management System") after Vertex had or should have learned of a similar failure of the load management system prior to October 2, YR-2.

III. Injuries

3.1   As a direct and proximate result of the negligence of defendant, plaintiff Raymond Garcia has suffered severe traumatic injuries, including, but not limited to, fractures to both of his legs and a closed head injury with an associated seizure disorder.

IV. Damages

4.1   As a direct and proximate result of the negligence of defendant, plaintiff Raymond Garcia has incurred medical expenses for treatment necessitated by these injuries and will continue to incur medical expenses in the future. As a further result of defendant's negligence, plaintiff has suffered pain, anguish, disability, loss of earnings, loss of earning capacity, and loss of ability to enjoy life, and will continue to sustain these damages in the future.

V. Prayer for Relief

WHEREFORE, the plaintiff, Raymond Garcia, prays for judgment against defendant for damages in a reasonable sum to be proved at trial, together with the taxable costs of this action, attorney's fees, and other relief as this Court deems proper.

DATED this 4th day of November, YR-2.

Repetto & Lincoln

Julia J. Repetto

JULIA J. REPETTO
Attorney at Law
5000 Logan Square
Nita City, Nita

In the Circuit Court of
Darrow County, Nita
Civil Division

RAYMOND GARCIA,   )

)   Civil Action

       Plaintiff,   )   CA 1948-IL

)

          v.   )   Answer

)

VERTEX MANUFACTURING COMPANY   )

)

       Defendant.   )

)

Defendant Vertex Manufacturing Company, answers plaintiff's complaint as follows:

1. Answering paragraph 1.1 of plaintiff's complaint, defendant is without knowledge or information sufficient to form a belief as to the truth of the allegations.

2. Answering paragraph 1.2 of plaintiff's complaint, defendant admits the same.

3. Answering paragraph 1.3 of plaintiff's complaint, defendant admits the same.

4. Answering paragraph 2.1, paragraph 2.2, paragraph 3.1 and paragraph 4.1 of plaintiff's complaint, defendant denies each and every allegation thereof.

First Affirmative Defense

Plaintiff's injuries, if any, were caused by his own negligence.

Second Affirmative Defense

Plaintiff's injury was proximately caused by the fault of persons or entities who are not parties to this action, including, but not limited to, Marine Resources Shipyard Corp., plaintiff's employer. Defendant's investigation is not complete and discovery is continuing.

WHEREFORE, having answered plaintiff's complaint and having pleaded its affirmative defenses, defendant asks the Court for relief as follows:

1. For dismissal of plaintiff's complaint with prejudice.

2. For recovery of its costs and attorney's fees herein.

DATED this 12th day of December, YR-2.

GILBERT, FOSNOT & BOSS

Eileen Gilbert

Eileen Gilbert
Attorneys for Defendants

DEPOSITION OF RAYMOND GARCIA
MAY 10, YR-1

1   My name is Raymond Garcia. I am thirty-four years old. I am the plaintiff in this action. I grew

2   up in an unincorporated rural area in Darrow County referred to as East Hill. I was raised by my

3   mom, Stella Garcia. My dad, who was a cop, and my mom divorced when I was two or three. He

4   left town for a job in Keetonville, Nita, and remarried. I saw him only a couple times a year.

5   I attended school here, graduating from East Hills High School in YR-17. I was never a particu-

6   larly good student, although I did pretty well in courses, like speech, that emphasized communica-

7   tion skills.

8   In grade school, my teachers complained to me and my mom about my "daydreaming" in class

9   sometimes. I admit that I was often bored and looked out the window, wishing I were doing some-

10   thing else. But, I never "zoned out," or had some kind of fit where I lost consciousness or anything

11   like that. I was just daydreaming.

12   I have a vague memory of being really sick when I was around five. I had a high fever and was

13   taken to the hospital by my mom, where I got shots. I used to get infected tonsils every spring be-

14   cause I have hay fever. After my tonsils were removed when I was six or seven, I didn't get sick like

15   that anymore.

16   My work history has kind of jumped around. I started out as a pizza cook after high school.

17   Then I worked in a warehouse for a while. Seemed like I was going no place, so I went down to

18   talk to an Army recruiter and ended up signing up. This didn't work out too well. Though I was

19   given an honorable discharge, they basically asked me to leave because I had a bad attitude. I guess

20   I wasn't mature enough to deal with military discipline. I attended some courses part-time at Nita

21   Community College after getting out of the Army. I got good grades—Bs—in real estate, writing,

22   and speech. But I had to stop, since I had to work full time. The NCC transcript I've been shown,

23   Exhibit 22, are the courses I took and the grades I got.

24   Over the last several years, I took some real estate courses at the community college and online,

25   courses like Real Estate Principles and Practices, Real Estate Finance, and Legal Aspects of Real

26   Estate. I took the Nita real estate salesperson license and passed about five years ago. After that, I

27   split my time between working at Marine Resources as a dry-dock rigger and selling real estate. I

28   worked at the shipyard for about seven years. Shipyard work is seasonal, so I filled in with the real

29   estate job when shipyard work was slow. Eventually, I want to open my own real estate office.

30   I was warned by Marine Resources several times for not showing up for work. The document

31   marked as Exhibit 27 shows that I was put on probation for absenteeism. Because I was showing

32   houses on the side, sometimes I'd have to miss work to show a house. It was tough to balance both

1   jobs. I was also warned in April of YR-3 for leaving work without permission. Again, I had business

2   to conduct and my boss wouldn't give me the day off, so I just left.

3   The tools I used as a rigger were personnel lifts, sand and water blasters, and welding, sanding

4   and painting equipment. I worked by myself some of the time, and other times with people who are

5   on my crew. It is pretty much a team effort at Marine Resources. I was assigned jobs at the begin-

6   ning of the shift by the lead person. I generally liked the work and the people there.

7   By the time of my accident, I had reached a point in my real estate career where I was starting

8   to get repeat business. People liked the fact that I always made the extra effort to answer their ques-

9   tions and to give full service. Most of my new listings and prospective buyers came from past client

10   referrals. The bad thing about real estate is that it fluctuates. Looking at the "Reported Earnings"

11   that my lawyer and I gave to the defense lawyer, you can see that some years I made next to noth-

12   ing, and other years I did quite well. In YR-4, I made close to $40,000 in real estate commissions.

13   But in YR-3, I only made about $5,000. YR-2, the year I was injured, was also kind of slow for real

14   estate. Up to the time of my accident, I had earned about $3,500. I haven't been able to go back to

15   it since then. The report of my earnings, Exhibit 25, is accurate.

16   I am not married now. I was divorced from my first wife Connie about four years prior to the

17   accident. We had no children. I don't know where she lives now. But it wasn't a nasty divorce or

18   anything like that. We just kind of fell out of love with one another. It was a mutual thing.

19   Right now I live with my girlfriend, Annie Rose, and her son, Fred, from a prior relationship.

20   She is on public assistance, but is in a community college training program and should be employed

21   soon. I don't have any dependents myself.

22   The accident, 10/2/YR-2, is a total blank. I know that we were working on a big cruise ship, the

23   Smorgasbord, at that time. I was painting it, working with John Machado in the Vertex personnel

24   lift. I don't recall anything else about that day. I like working with John as he is well respected and

25   has been a lead man for years. We occasionally have a beer or two after work, but we don't socialize

26   other than that. He's an older guy, married with lots of kids at home. He's been at the yard about

27   fifteen years, I think.

28   Prior to the accident, we did have safety training at Marine Resources. Melvin Demsky did the

29   training. They specifically have personnel lift training. You learn how to operate them, the safety

30   do's and don'ts. I am personnel lift certified, that's what they called it at Marine Resources. That

31   means I've been through Demsky's training. I recall him teaching us about how we were supposed

32   to inspect these lifts' safety systems, including the one that prevents tipping over, before we used the

33   lifts. I think there is a decal on them that tells you how to do it. I really don't much about personnel

34   lifts, other than how to operate them. I don't recall ever seeing a manual for that lift.

35   Demsky taught us about the lights on the control panel. The photo of the control panel you've

36   shown me, Exhibit 9, looks like that of the lift I was in when it fell. If the lights in the lower left of

1   the panel were blue or yellow, you were safe. If the light was solid red, you could still work in the
2   lift, but you were near to tipping over. You were OK until the red light began blinking and an alarm
3   sounded. Then you had to either raise the bucket or shorten the boom, or both. I didn't use the 110-
4   foot lift too much, but I never saw or heard of one tipping over at the shipyard. I don't recall ever
5   being in the 110 footer when the red light blinked and the alarm went off. If we needed to move to
6   work horizontally, we usually moved the whole lift.

7   I can't remember anything about the tip-over warning lights on the control panel in the basket
8   on the day I was injured. I do know that if the red light ever started blinking and the alarm went
9   off, John and I would have stopped whatever we were doing and boomed in real fast.

10   Yes, the photos of the yellow decals with the operating instructions and daily inspection proce-
11 dures, Exhibits 10, 11, 18, and 19, look like the ones on the 110-foot lift that fell. Frankly, I learned
12 from the other workers that it was not necessary to do all that complicated and time-consuming
13 stuff that Demsky instructed us to do. We usually inspected the lifts at the beginning of the day, but
14 not before every shift. Every morning, we'd start the lift up and do a "walk around" inspection. You
15 know, to see if there were any fluid leaks, obvious damage, or if it wasn't operating normal. If we
16 were taking the lift from an earlier shift, we'd rely on them to tell us if there was something wrong
17 with it. If it was operating OK for them, we didn't inspect it. If any problems developed with the
18 lifts, Marine Resources called the manufacturer, Vertex, to come fix them.

19   There are regular safety meetings at Marine Resources every other Thursday. They'd last about
20 twenty to thirty minutes. We'd talk about wearing hard hats and safety glasses, looking out for mov-
21 ing forklifts in the yard, staying away from electrical lines, wearing ear protection, those kinds of
22 things. We didn't use the 110-foot lifts a lot at Marine Resources. The typical equipment around
23 there was between 40 and 60 feet. I don't remember if there have been any other tip-over accidents
24 at work.

25   I know that I was on the swing shift, from 4:00 p.m. to 12:00 a.m., when I was hurt. I had
26 been on that shift for some time. I would have had on a hard hat and maybe put on a paper suit to
27 protect my clothes from the overspray. We were using paint rollers with long handles. There was a
28 paint pump on the dock with lines that ran up to the power roller. There was no other equipment
29 in the basket that I can remember, nor would there be.

30   Otherwise, the day of the accident is a blank. I remember waking up at Memorial Hospital the
31 next day. I didn't know where I was. My legs felt heavy. Somebody told me that they were broken
32 and that I had been involved in an accident. I found out later that both my ankles had been oper-
33 ated on. My lower legs were in a cast. I had severe pain in my head, back, left hip, and left shoulder.
34 Any light at all hurt my eyes and head, and I was seeing double for weeks.

35   I was told that I had a frontal lobe head injury. There was a gash three or four inches long on
36 the left top side of my head that required fifteen to twenty stitches. The picture you have shown

1   me, Exhibit 26, is of my stitches. There was also a circular gash on the backside of my head. I was

2   in constant pain. The pain medicine helped only a little.

3   I left Memorial Hospital three days after the accident. I also required some home nursing care,

4   particularly when transferring from the wheelchair to the commode and other places. I've had

5   physical and occupational therapy. I still walk with some difficulty. The pain still has not gone away

6   entirely. I often have a slight ringing in my left ear. It drives me crazy.

7   There have been no other on-the-job injuries in my work at Marine Resources.

8   The worst problems since the tip-over on October 2 have to do with my head injury. A lot of

9   times I feel like I'm going crazy now. I don't want to leave the house. I think something bad is going

10 to happen to me. I don't like to be around other people too much.

11   Panic attacks come on me randomly now. My heart starts racing and sweat breaks out on my

12 forehead. I can't seem to concentrate on anything. My girlfriend Annie and my mom tell me that

13 they ask me questions and my mind seems to be someplace else, like I've totally spaced out. I have

14 no memory of it happening. It never happened before the accident. It kind of scares me.

15   Dr. Moretti, a neurologist at Memorial Hospital, did an EEG test on me while I was in the hos-

16 pital and believes that I have a seizure disorder as a result of this accident. Dr. Moretti had started

17 me on Dilantin. I have also seen a neuropsychologist, Dr. Arbogast after the tip-over accident.

18   All the services I have received from outpatient rehab at Memorial Hospital since the tip-over

19 at Marine Resources have been a big help. Even so, despite taking the medication, I don't feel that

20 I can ever go back to work again. I find it hard to just get through from one day to the next. I am

21 thankful that my family has been supportive, as has Annie.

22   While I did have some problems with anger management in the past, this was no longer true

23 after I took some classes following an incident involving Annie four years ago. We got into an argu-

24 ment over money. I bought a new shotgun and she thought I had spent the money we'd been saving

25 for her son's Christmas present. We got into it pretty good. Finally, she attacked me and I had to

26 push her off and hold her down until she calmed down. Well, the cops were called, and you know

27 how it goes, it's always the guy's fault when a domestic violence complaint is filed. I pled guilty to

28 simple assault and was put on probation and ordered to take an anger management course. My

29 philosophy is that it takes two to make a fight. But I regret that it happened and I did find the anger

30 management classes helpful. The best proof of this is that Annie and I are still together and doing

31 well.

32   But I never had the kind of self-control problems that I am now. Most days, I don't even want to

33 get up in the morning. I know it's just going to be more panic attacks, depression, and isolation.

This deposition was taken in the office of defendant's counsel on May 10, YR-1. This deposition was given under oath and was read and signed by the deponent.

Certified by:

Penelope Harrison

_____

Penelope Harrison
Certified Shorthand Reporter
(CSR)

DEPOSITION OF JOHN MACHADO
MAY 5, YR-1

1   My name is John Machado. I live at Cascade Apartments, No. 150, 1048 Fifth Avenue, Nita

2   City, Nita 55520. I am fifty-two years old and married. I have five children. I work as a dock rigger

3   for Marine Resources Shipyard and have worked there for twelve years. I work on the ships that

4   come to the yard for refitting or repair. That might include knocking off rust, painting, and repair-

5   ing or replacing obsolete, broken, or damaged equipment on the ships. I do a lot of painting, sand-

6   ing, power cleaning, and welding. Often we have to work in a basket on a lift that is on the dock. It

7   is hard, dirty, and sometimes dangerous work, but I like it.

8   I was in the lift basket with Ray Garcia on October 2, YR-2 when it fell. I operated the controls.

9   When Ray and I reported for work on the afternoon shift that day, we were assigned to continue the

10   painting of the Smorgasbord, which was in the dry dock. We had to use the 110-foot Vertex lift to

11   reach the areas that needed painting. The 110-footer was being used by the guys on the prior shift

12   to do some welding on the ship's railings. They told us that they had tested the lift that morning and

13   it was operating just fine. If anything unusual had happened to the lift during the day shift, they

14   would have told us, as we look out for one another.

15   I was operating the lift from the control panel in the basket. Ray was beside me. We each had

16   powered paint rollers that had tubes connected to barrels of paint on the dock. A pump on the dock

17   pumps paint up the tubes to the handle of the roller and to the roller. It is tricky to maneuver the

18   basket and not run afoul of the paint lines, but I had no problems that day.

19   We had been working for about a half an hour. I had to move the basket a couple times to get to

20   new areas to be painted. I don't think I had moved the base unit of the lift yet. But while I was again

21   booming out and over, all of a sudden the basket began to flutter like a leaf and began plummeting

22   downward. We must have fallen about seventy-five feet.

23   There was no warning that we were about to tip over. We were taught that a light on the lower

24   left of the control panel, shown in Exhibit 9, would start blinking red and an alarm would sound

25   if the boom and basket had reached its limit and that a tip-over was going to happen if you didn't

26   either raise the basket or boom in. When I use that lift, I always make sure that either the blue or

27   yellow light is lit. With less than 500 pounds in the basket, it is OK as long as the red light isn't

28   blinking and the alarm isn't sounding. Ray, me, and our equipment that day weighed less than 500

29   pounds.

30   There was no warning horn or blinking red light when the basket fell on October 2, YR-2. I

31   can't recall which of the colored lights was shining when we fell, but I know I didn't hear or see any

32   tip-over warning. I'm not stupid. We were seventy to eighty feet up. I wouldn't continue to boom

1   out while the warnings are going off. I'd stop and boom in. That's one reason why I've been able to
2   do this job for twelve years with no serious injuries.

3   The shipyard bought the Vertex 110 only about a month before this accident, so I had used it
4   only a few times. Normally, I had used the 60-foot Vertex lift. It is steady as a rock. I don't think it
5   even has a tip-over warning.

6   We were trained by Mr. Demsky at Marine Resources about the tip-over warning system the
7   110 footer has and how to check it out. He also gives us general safety reminders every other week
8   (like, follow all instructions on the machine's decals, watch out for people and power lines when
9   moving equipment, report problems with equipment, especially safety equipment like harnesses
10   and back-up warning alarms). However, we dock riggers on the second shift at Marine Resources
11   often don't test the anti-tip-over system again after they've already done it on the day shift and not
12   had any problems during the shift.

13   Before this accident, we never had a lift tip over. The guys using the 110-foot lift on the shift be-
14   fore us told Ray and me that it was working fine. We assumed the lift had been properly maintained
15   and was working right. If there was a problem with the tip-over warning, I assumed the red light
16   would blink and the horn would sound, or the boom controls wouldn't operate. We were never told
17   that the lights on the control panel would light as usual and the boom would operate even though
18   the tip-over warning system was knocked out. To me, that's pretty stupid—and dangerous.

19   There are lots of power lines around when working on a ship. Ships are deep, dark places. When
20   they are dry docked like the Smorgasbord, the crew is gone and the ship's power is shut down.
21   You need lots of lights and power tools when working inside. When working in a lift on the dock
22   alongside a ship, we stay clear of these power lines. Sometimes we have to move them so we can get
23   access to the ship. On October 2, YR-2, the boom or basket didn't hit any power lines, although I'm
24   sure some were in the general area. But, before we fell, nothing unusual happened. I was not aware
25   that power lines or power equipment could short out the lift's anti-tip-over system. Nevertheless, I
26   always try to steer the boom and basket clear of them.

27   On impact, I seriously hurt my back and left leg. I never lost consciousness and began to scream
28   for help. After a few minutes, safety people from Marine Resources arrived. They called for an out-
29   side ambulance. As we waited for its arrival, Chet Pinole, an MRS supervisor, asked me how the
30   accident occurred and how I was doing. The two photos identified as Exhibits 7 and 8 are accurate
31   pictures of the lift after the fall. I've also seen the computer-animated pictures of how the lift fell
32   (Exhibits 20a–c), and they look accurate too.

33   Ray Garcia was knocked out for about eight or ten minutes at this point. During the next ten
34   minutes, he slipped in and out of consciousness at least four times. At one point he got crazy, all
35   hyper, jumped up, started tearing off his clothes and trying to move around. He had to be forced
36   back down to the ground.

1   We were transported to Memorial Hospital in separate ambulances. The next time I saw him

2   was about two weeks later, when he was being released from the hospital. He got a bad head injury

3   and couldn't remember anything about the accident. I didn't. I was lucky. Poor guy. Now he can't

4   work anymore at the shipyard.

5   I worked with Ray Garcia at the shipyard for several years. He was a little hot-headed and had

6   some absence from work issues, but was a good worker. I think he was dabbling in real estate on the

7   side. I've never known him to "space out" on me. We didn't socialize much, only had a beer or two

8   together after work occasionally. He always seemed like a normal guy to me. He was a sober worker,

9   and I think he was living with his girlfriend when the accident happened.

    This deposition was taken in the office of defendant's counsel on May 5, YR-1. This deposition
was given under oath, and was read and signed by the deponent.

Certified by:

Penelope Harrison

_____

Penelope Harrison
Certified Shorthand Reporter
(CSR)

DEPOSITION OF WERNER GERHARD, PE
JUNE 8, YR-1

1   My name is Werner Gerhard. I am forty-four years old. I am currently self-employed as a fo-
2   rensic consulting engineer doing business as Precision Failure Analysis. I have a bachelor's degree in
3   mechanical engineering from Purdue University, with a specialization in control systems. I initially
4   worked on defense projects for the Boeing Company for six years, with emphasis on computer
5   simulation and control system development and analysis.

6   I have had extensive experience in designing and analyzing electronic control systems for indus-
7   trial tooling and equipment, similar to the load management safety system in the Vertex personnel
8   lift that tipped over on October 2, YR-2. I have never been involved in the design of a personnel
9   lift and do not know what that industry's specifications are for control systems of this type. I do not
10 know how the Vertex lift here compares with other lifts in the industry.

11 On October 2, YR-2, my company was contacted by Marine Resources and hired to investigate
12 a lift accident that occurred earlier that afternoon. The report of my October 3 and 4 investiga-
13 tion at Marine Resources is dated October 22, YR-2. Marine Resources produced it to Mr. Garcia's
14 counsel and defense counsel. I have a copy with me.

15 After that report was filed, I was also present on January 23, YR-1, when Marvin Felix, a Vertex
16 quality and safety engineering employee, performed tests on two circuit cards in the lift's load man-
17 agement system (LMS). These tests indicated that neither circuit card was functional. I subsequently
18 reviewed the wiring diagrams for the load management system and the schematics and drawings for
19 the system's circuit cards, which were provided by Vertex. I tested the circuit cards to determine how
20 they failed. The photos you've shown me, Exhibits 12 and 15, appear to be the circuit boards that
21 were in the Vertex 110 Personnel Lift's load management system that I examined at the shipyard in
22 October. The simplified wire diagram now being shown to me, Exhibit 2, is an accurate diagram of
23 the electrical circuits and connections between the two boards in the Vertex 110's LMS.

24 The load management system was designed to prevent the lift from tipping over. The boom can
25 be extended 110 feet and raised or lowered to various positions, ranging from 90 degrees vertical to
26 completely horizontal. Extending or lowering the boom increases the load on the base of the boom,
27 and if it is moved beyond its designed operating range, the lift will tip over.

28 The load management system senses an imminent tip-over through two electrical switches, a
29 "mechanical" switch and a "proximity" switch, that are located on the turret above the lift's base
30 between large springs. As the boom load increases, the springs compress and the switches move
31 closer to the base. Before the boom can actually tip over, the mechanical switch is activated when

1   its plunger makes physical contact with the base. The proximity switch is activated when its sensor

2   comes within range of a metallic "target" on the personnel lift base.

3   When either circuit card receives a signal from its respective switch, it activates the load man-

4   agement systems warning horn and flashing red light and cuts off power to the boom so it can't be

5   extended or lowered any further. This prevents the boom from moving into an actual tip-over posi-

6   tion. The cards shown in Exhibit 12 are the circuit cards that appeared not to be functioning when

7   tested by Mr. Felix on January 23, YR-1.

8   I conducted a series of tests to determine which specific components of these circuit cards had

9   failed. Mr Felix allowed me to take possession of the circuit cards that he removed from the Vertex

10   110 in question. I ordered a new circuit card from Vertex to use as an exemplar and attached it to

11   a mechanical switch of the type used in the lift's load management system. It is pictured in Exhibit

12   13, which I took. I then tripped the switch and simulated an electrical overload condition. This

13   caused the circuit card to fail. I took voltage readings from the card's components and was able to

14   isolate the failure to one transistor.

15   I next replaced the exemplar circuit card with one of the original circuit cards from the person-

16   nel lift and repeated the simulated overload. All the voltage readings fell within the expected range

17   except for the same transistor that failed on the exemplar card.

18   After these tests were completed, I removed the two transistors on the original and exemplar

19   cards that had not given the expected voltage readings and tested each for internal damage. My

20   testing revealed that each transistor had been burned out and rendered nonfunctional as the result

21   of the electrical overload. The failure of these transistors made it impossible for the circuit cards to

22   transmit the current that activates the warning horn and blinking light, and disables the boom. This

23   is the reason why the load management system failed to function at the time of the accident.

24   Moreover, Vertex's wiring diagram shows that these two circuit cards lacked true redundancy.

25   The circuit cards have a common connection to each other and to the horn in the ground control

26   station. The circuit cards failed simultaneously, due to a random, external electrical overload that

27   was transmitted from one card to the other through the common connection. It is not possible that

28   an external overload could have caused only one of the cards to fail and not the other, given the fact

29   that they are connected at a common point.

30   Due to the large number of potential external sources of the electrical overload that could cause

31   the cards to fail, such as coming close to power lines or the workers in the basket operating power

32   equipment, and the random nature of such overload occurrences, the probability that both circuit

33   cards failed a day or a month before the accident is no greater than the probability that they failed

34   five minutes or an instant before the accident. It is therefore pure speculation to claim that testing

35   the load management system on the day of the accident, or even before the injured workers' shift,

36   would have resulted in the discovery that the circuit cards had failed. The overload that burned out

1   these transistors could have existed for a very short period of time. There was no discoloration on

2   the transistors that came from the lift in question that would indicate heat was developing over a

3   long period of time.

4   The design of the load management system in the Vertex 110 lift is also defective and dangerous

5   because the people working in the basket would have had no way to know when these two transis-

6   tors blew. As designed, the solid blue, yellow, and solid red lights on the control panel would operate

7   as normal even though the circuit cards had failed. The design of the LMS should have incorporated

8   some way of warning the lift operators that the LMS was not functioning.

9   This would have been easy. Either a visual or audible warning could have been designed into

10   the system to be tripped whenever the circuit cards ceased functioning for whatever reason. In your

11   car, for instance, a red light tells you when the trunk or a door is not fully closed. The car won't

12   start if it is not in "park" and your foot is on the brake. It has a "check engine" light on the dash.

13   An alarm tells you that you forgot to fasten your seatbelt. The cost to the manufacturer of adding

14   such a safety precaution would be minimal and might have prevented this accident. In my opinion,

15   it is not a reasonably safe design for this lift to be operable when the LMS is not functioning, or, at

16   least, without a warning that it is malfunctioning. This is especially so when the cards are not truly

17   redundant. As a result, you can't rely on one switch to do the job when the other has shorted out.

18   There is no backup system to protect the workers.

19   While I was doing my investigation and testing, I learned of another Vertex personnel lift ac-

20   cident in YR-5, where the same circuit cards malfunctioned. I learned about this from Mr. Felix,

21   Vertex's quality control and safety engineer.

22   I also learned that after that YR-5 tip-over, the circuit cards in the load management system

23   were redesigned. They now have an automatically resetting fuse. One is shown in Exhibit 14. The

24   new and old circuit cards are shown side-by-side in Exhibit 15. That is, when a power surge or a

25   short circuit occurs, the new card has a fuse that trips and cuts all electrical power to the cards so

26   there will be no damage to the cards' transistors. This is like a circuit breaker in your house. And,

27   after the fuse is tripped, it automatically resets itself after five minutes. The theory is that after five

28   minutes, the short or overload will have passed and it is safe to, in effect, open the circuit cards to

29   electrical signals from the two tip-over switches. If these new redesigned cards had been in the per-

30   sonnel lift on October 2, YR-2, it could have prevented the tip-over. At least, the new cards would

31   have limited the time when the lift was functioning without its tip-over warning system in opera-

32   tion to just five minutes.

33   Though this new system is still defectively designed because it lacks true redundancy and be-

34   cause it still fails for about five minutes to warn the lift operator that the anti-tip-over system has

35   ceased to work, at least the resetting fuse would act as a Band-Aid to prevent damage to the tran-

36   sistors in the load management system's circuit cards. But this does not render it a reasonably safe

1   design, in my opinion, because the workers still would not be aware that they are working without

2   a functioning anti-tip-over system for up to five full minutes. There is no excuse for this to be so.

This deposition was taken in the office of plaintiff's counsel on June 8, YR-1. This deposition was given under oath, and was read and signed by the deponent.

Certified by:

Penelope Harrison

_____

Penelope Harrison
Certified Shorthand Reporter
(CSR)

DEPOSITION OF MELVIN DEMSKY
JUNE 23, YR-1

1   My name is Melvin Demsky. I am thirty-eight years old and have been employed by Marine

2 Resources Shipyard for twenty years. I am a high school and junior college graduate. After high

3 school, I started at MRS as a dry-dock worker, called a "dock rigger." I am currently in charge of

4 occupational safety and health at the shipyard. I have taken over twenty different courses in worker

5 health and safety the ten years I have held my current position. I have never received any formal

6 training in the safe use of personnel lifts like the Vertex 110.

7   My job is to make sure the occupational safety and health regulations are complied with by the

8 MRS workers. I conduct the training on how to properly and safely operate all of our equipment,

9 from sandblasters and power washers to personnel lifts and cranes. I use both classroom instruction

10 and hands-on training. The usual training session lasts anywhere from twenty minutes to an hour.

11   My job requires me to learn all about any new equipment we get and train the workers how

12 to operate it properly and safely. One of the most important aspects of worker safety training is to

13 teach the workers how to properly inspect the equipment before using it.

14   When we acquired the Vertex 110 personnel lift about a month before the accident involving

15 Machado and Garcia, I studied the owner's manual and tested the lift personally. I noticed that this

16 lift, unlike the 60-foot Vertex lifts that we already owned, had a "load management system," which

17 is just a fancy name for its tip-over prevention and warning system. This is because when the boom

18 is extended beyond fifty feet and angled so the basket is more than fifty feet from the base horizon-

19 tally, the weight of the boom and the basket, together with the weight of the workers and equip-

20 ment in the basket, put a great deal of leverage on the lift's base, creating a serious risk of tipping

21 over the base. The load management system is designed both to warn the workers in the basket that

22 a tip-over is imminent with a blinking red light and a siren, and to prevent a tip-over by making it

23 impossible to increase the leverage by booming out or down. This is explained on the basket and

24 the base control panels below the three LMS lights at the lower left of the panel, as illustrated in the

25 lift's manual and marked as Exhibit 1f.

26   I held a thirty-minute training session on the Vertex 110 for all the dock riggers a couple of

27 days after we received it. Exhibit 3 is the training checklist I used. This included John Machado and

28 Ray Garcia. I impressed upon them that this lift could easily tip over and told them about the anti-

29 tip-over system and how to check that it was working properly before using the lift. I pointed out

30 the decal on the base's control panel that describes the steps to take to test the anti-tip-over system,

31 now being shown to me and marked as Exhibit 11, and showed them the load limits diagram and

32 indicator lights on both control panels and what they mean. I told all of the shifts at their training

1   sessions that if they were going to boom out more than about fifty feet, they should first check the

2   tip-over safety system before using the lift. Also, we adopted a straight 500 pound load limit for the

3   basket at all times, even though the lift could easily handle up to a 1000 pounds when in the "green

4   light" zone.

5   Then, I showed them how to test the LMS; how toggling the "P" switch on the base control

6   panel while doing the boom-out test tested the "Proximity" safety switch, and toggling the "M"

7   switch tested the "Mechanical" safety switch. Then I had a few workers actually do the test. I told

8   them that if the boom did not stop where it was supposed to when tested that meant the anti-tip-

9   over system wasn't working properly, and that they should not use the lift. They should call the

10   maintenance yard to take the lift off the dock for repairs.

11   Before this accident I was not aware that there were two circuit cards in the load management

12   system, or even where they were. Our maintenance people would not know how to fix the load

13   management system on this lift. They'd have to call Vertex or a Vertex-authorized repair facility.

14   Vertex offered to train our mechanics how to inspect and repair the 110 lift, including the LMS,

15   but we had not gotten around to sending anyone to this training prior to this accident. Since the

16   accident, we have sent an MRS mechanic to be trained at Vertex.

17   I am aware that power surges could knock out the LMS. I'm not sure if I told the workers this

18   during my training sessions. However, I was not aware that the boom would continue to function

19   normally and the blue, yellow, and red load indicator lights on the control panel would continue

20   to illuminate even though the LMS was not functioning. Consequently, I did not warn the work-

21   ers about this when I trained them. I guess that if I had known this, I would have been even more

22   insistent that they test the LMS before every use.

23   I am aware that our workers do not actually test the load management system before using the

24   lift. Several times before the accident, I went onto the dock and asked the workers using the 110 lift

25   if they had checked the anti-tip-over system. They had not. I'd chew them out and require they test

26   it right then and there before using it again. Believe me, they were pretty unhappy. But, since no-

27   body had come close to tipping over in that lift up to that point, I guess the workers thought testing

28   the LMS was a waste of time. They get complacent—until someone gets hurt, like John and Ray.

29   Since the accident, I've been telling the riggers about what happened to Ray and John to emphasize

30   the importance of testing the LMS before using the lift, every time. Now the workers are checking

31   out the LMS pretty regularly, but still, some just forget or refuse to do it because it takes time to do

32   it. I try to keep after them about it, but, well, I can't be everywhere all time.

This deposition was taken in the office of plaintiff's counsel on June 23, YR-1. This deposition was given under oath, and was read and signed by the deponent.

Certified by:

Penelope Harrison

_____

Penelope Harrison
Certified Shorthand Reporter
(CSR)

DEPOSITION OF MARVIN FELIX
APRIL 25, YR-1

1   My name is Marvin Felix. I am thirty-six years old. I am currently employed as product reli-
2   ability and safety engineer with Vertex, Inc. This company is the world leader in the manufacturing
3   of aerial work platforms, such as the one involved in this case.

4   I have a bachelor of science degree in engineering from Texas A & M University. I took courses
5   in all aspects of engineering, mechanical, civil, and electrical. After graduation from college, I went
6   to work for Vertex. I started out as a design engineer, and after that, I went into product safety.

7   On a day-to-day basis, I am in contact with our customers and all the engineering departments
8   at Vertex. I regularly go out in the field and watch our machines operate. I am involved with our
9   design teams regularly. I help to develop safety manuals, videos, and product literature. I have
10   six engineers working under me. I also am the company representative to the American National
11   Standards Institute.

12   Whenever there is any question about the safety of any of our products out in the field, I person-
13   ally investigate it. We are committed to providing safe and reliable equipment that meets or exceeds
14   the industry standards. I visit our dealers on a somewhat regular basis to see what is going on, what
15   complaints, if any, they are hearing from the users of our products. There is also a yearly gathering
16   of all our dealers in which we discuss the performance and safety aspects of our equipment.

17   The Vertex 110 personnel lift involved in this case was first introduced by our company in
18   YR-10. It is still being manufactured today. We have built and sold approximately 500 of these
19   machines at this point. The Vertex 110 is used in a wide variety of applications, both industrial set-
20   tings, as well as construction and maritime. It has been very reliable in the field from an operation
21   and safety standpoint. There has been only one other tip-over type accident besides this one. That
22   occurred at a power plant in Hoboken, New Jersey, on August 26, YR-5. I personally investigated
23   what happened in that situation. Exhibit 5 is my report of that investigation. Both of the circuit
24   cards on the load management were not functioning because of improper maintenance by the
25   owner of the lift, which caused a short circuit. Also, the person using the lift did not check out the
26   lift's load management system prior to using it. Like in this case, had the testing of the LMS been
27   done prior to use, as the decal on the lift instructs, the faulty circuit cards would have been discov-
28   ered and the accident prevented.

29   I inspected the Vertex 110 lift involved in this accident on two occasions, December 12, YR-2,
30   and January 23, YR-1. An independent investigator hired by the shipyard, a Mr. Werner Gerhard,
31   was present during my second inspection when I examined the lift's circuit cards. I have reviewed
32   Gerhard's report. It is accurate insofar as it describes the Vertex 110's functions, and I have no

1 quarrel with his description of the condition of the lift on the dock after it tipped over. However,
2 I disagree with some of his conclusions. Please see my written report, marked as Exhibit 4, for my
3 findings based on my initial investigation.

4   During the second inspection, which was more detailed, I found that the two switches on the
5 load management system were not functioning properly due to the circuit cards being damaged.
6 They are both pictured in Exhibit 12. When the boom is extended too far to operate safely, one or
7 both of the switches in the load management system will send an electrical signal to their respective
8 circuit card. When this occurs, the red load radius light on the lower left of the control panels in
9 the basket and on the turret will flash and an alarm will sound. These lights are shown at the lower
10 left of the control panel in the picture marked as Exhibit 9, and in the illustration of the control
11 panel in the lift's manual. The boom down and telescope out functions are rendered nonfunctional
12 until such time as the operator moves the boom into a safe position. Because both circuit cards were
13 damaged, the tip-over warning and prevention functions were not working at all.

14   It is true that strong external electrical currents can cause an electrical overload in the LMS and
15 short out a circuit card. It is hard for me to tell exactly what level of electrical currents were present
16 at Marine Resources on the day of the accident, as they were not tested at that time and I did not
17 search for any on the day of the accident. However, given my general knowledge of industrial work-
18 place conditions from many, many site visits in the course of working at Vertex, I know that these
19 had to be very strong to knock out the electronics of the load management system.

20   The failure of the cards would have been discovered here if the injured workers had bothered to
21 check the load management system at the beginning of their shift. If they had, this accident would
22 have been prevented.

23   If an external electrical source encountered after the workers began using the lift caused the fail-
24 ure of the LMS circuit cards, then there is either a lack of employee training by Marine Resources on
25 avoiding external electric power sources, or else the workers failed to heed such training and avoid
26 sources of electric surges. There is an explicit warning regarding external electrical sources on the
27 control panel of the lift. It is shown in Exhibit 19, under "Electrocution Hazard."

28   The design of our load management system meets or exceeds applicable industry standards.
29 Safety redundancy is built into this system with written warnings and warning lights on the con-
30 trol panel, an audible alarm, and an automatic boom function lock-out. Even the best designed
31 mechanical device needs to be serviced and checked regularly, particularly when put to hard use
32 in an industrial setting. Look at the pictures of this lift's control panel taken at the accident scene,
33 such as Exhibits 9 and 17! Also, Marine Resources could have sent their mechanics to our factory
34 school to learn how best to maintain and repair this lift. They didn't do so until after this accident
35 happened.

1   The circuit cards on our load management system have been changed in two or three small ways
2   since the Vertex 110 that Marine Resources owns came on the market. The most significant change
3   to this card was to add—made after Marine Resources bought the lift, but before the Garcia acci-
4   dent—was that we added what I call an automatic resetting fuse. That change was based on input
5   we received from our customers. It is shown in Exhibit 14. Whenever these circuit cards shorted out
6   for whatever reason, it would always show up in the daily preoperation checks. However, changing
7   out a damaged circuit card involved some downtime for the machine. With the resetting fuse, the
8   fuse automatically reset itself after about five minutes, assuming the overload condition had ended.
9   The circuit card did not have to be replaced. As a result, the lift had much less downtime and own-
10   ers did not have to replace the cards as often. Now, owners only have to replace resetting fuse circuit
11   cards if they are damaged so badly that they will not reset automatically or manually. I can't say
12   whether any external sources of electricity on the dock at Marine Resources would have been strong
13   enough to do this much damage.

14   Because we did not add this resetting fuse to the circuit card for safety reasons, we did not send
15   out a service bulletin to our customers or recall the product. We already had the best anti-tip-over
16   protection in the industry with our redundant backup systems. All the checks and balances in this
17   product had proven successful in the past. The new circuit card did not change in any way the un-
18   derlying function of the load management system itself. Nor did it change the requirement posted
19   on the lift's yellow decal, Exhibit 10, that the load management system be tested daily before using
20   the lift.

21   Vertex has an expectation that the mechanics working on our products and those using them
22   will be properly trained and responsible. We have put out a safe product with proper instructions
23   and warnings. The people who purchase the machines have an obligation to follow our recom-
24   mended procedures. One of the workers at MR has admitted that they frequently don't bother to
25   test the LMS before using the lift. This accident is entirely the fault of Marine Resources and its
26   workers.

27   Based on my experience, training, and familiarity with the Vertex 110, I can state that if the
28   Marine Resources workers had tested the load management system on this machine every time it
29   was to be used, as we require, the problems with the circuit cards would have been discovered and
30   this accident would not have occurred.

31   It is true that the load management system does not automatically warn the user of the lift that
32   the anti-tip-over safety systems (the blinking red light and siren) are nonfunctional for any reason.
33   It is also true that the load management indicator lights, the green, yellow, and solid red lights on
34   the control panel, continue to work even if the anti-tip-over warning and prevention mechanisms
35   are not working. This is for safety reasons.

1   If all of the load indicator lights stopped functioning too when the circuit cards connected to
2   the warning and lock-out mechanism are shorted out, the workers would not know in which load
3   zone they were. Thus, as it is now, even with the warning and lock out mechanism down, the work-
4   ers are guided by the green, yellow, and red lights to stay within a safe working zone.

5   We assume that when a worker finds himself in the solid red light zone, he won't continue to
6   boom out or down and make the risk of a tip-over even more severe. We find that most workers
7   are careful to keep the boom and basket in the green light or yellow light zone, and stay away from
8   the solid red light zone. Therefore, we did not think it necessary to design the anti-tip-over system
9   so that all the lights would go out when it is malfunctioning, or to have it give some other type of
10   warning to the lift user that this safety system was not functioning. We believe that testing the tip-
11   over warning and prevention before each use is sufficient protection of users of the lift.

12   As for Mr. Gerhard's opinion that the two circuit cards in the tip-over warning and prevention
13   system are not truly redundant, I disagree. I think we have different meanings of "redundant."
14   I mean that the lift has two independent ways in which it can detect an imminent tip-over: the
15   proximity and the mechanical switches. If one of these switches is not tripped, but the other is, the
16   audible warning and lock out occur. The system is also redundant in that there are two warnings:
17   the blinking light and the siren. It is further redundant in that when tripped, the safety system also
18   makes it impossible to boom out or down. This provides extra safety to the users of the lift. It's like
19   having two or three smoke detectors in your house. If, for any reason, one is either not working or
20   the triggering condition has not yet reached one of them, the other may be tripped anyway.

21   I understand that Mr. Gerhard is saying that both circuit cards could possibly be shorted out
22   at the same time by an external electrical overload because they have a common connection at the
23   siren. But, in my experience, that does not happen often enough to have justified the expense of
24   redesigning the card wiring shown in the lift's manual.

This deposition was taken in the office of defendant's counsel on April 25, YR-1. This deposition was given under oath, and was read and signed by the deponent.

Certified by:

Penelope Harrison

_____

Penelope Harrison
Certified Shorthand Reporter
(CSR)

FROM THE VERTEX 110 PERSONNEL LIFT MANUAL

FROM THE VERTEX 110 PERSONNEL LIFT MANUAL

SECTION 2 — PREPARATION AND INSPECTION

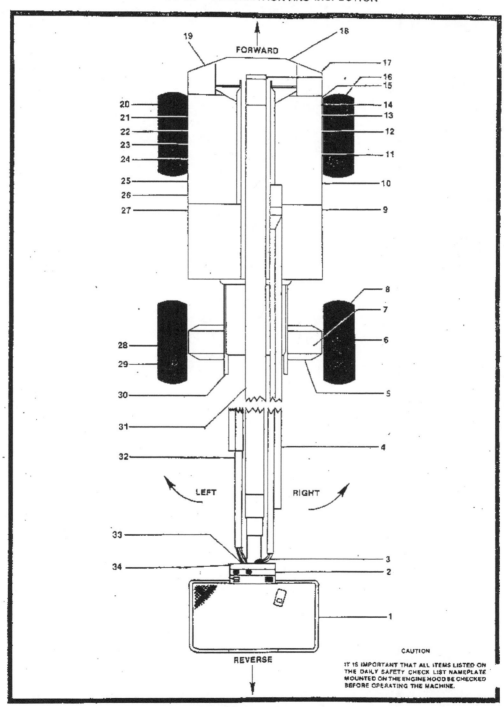

Figure 2-1. Daily Walkaround Inspection.(Sheet 1 of 2)

CAUTION

IT IS IMPORTANT THAT ALL ITEMS LISTED ON THE DAILY SAFETY CHECK LIST NAMEPLATE MOUNTED ON THE ENGINE HOOD BE CHECKED BEFORE OPERATING THE MACHINE.

FROM THE VERTEX 110 PERSONNEL LIFT MANUAL

SECTION 2 — PREPARATION AND INSPECTION

GENERAL.

The most efficient method of checking your machine is by conducting a "Walk-Around Inspection".

Begin your "Walk-Around Inspection" at Item 1, as noted on the diagram. Continue to your right (counterclockwise viewed from top) checking each item in sequence for the conditions listed in the "Walk-Around Inspection Checklist".

WARNING

TO AVOID INJURY DO NOT OPERATE MACHINE UNTIL ALL MALFUNCTIONS HAVE BEEN CORRECTED. USE OF A MALFUNCTIONING MACHINE IS A SAFETY VIOLATION.

CAUTION

TO AVOID POSSIBLE INJURY, BE SURE MACHINE POWER IS "OFF". DURING "WALK-AROUND INSPECTION."

Note

Do not overlook visual inspection of chassis underside. Checking this area often results in discovery of conditions which could cause extensive machine damage.

1. Platform Assembly - No loose or missing parts; no visible damage. Lock pins/bolts in place. Foot-switch in good working order; not modified, disabled, or blocked.
2. Platform Control Console - Switches and levers properly secured; no loose or missing parts; visible damage; placards secured and legible; levers and switches return to neutral. Control markings legible.
3. Hose and Cable Guards/Clamps - Properly secured; no visible damage.
4. Power Track - No loose, damaged, or missing parts; hydraulic and electrical lines - no visible damage.
5. Drive Motor and Brake, Right Rear - no visible damage; evidence of leakage.
6. Drive Hub, Right Rear - No visible damage; evidence of leakage.
7. Extendable Axle - Lock pins in place, properly secured. Check both sides.
8. Drive Wheel/Tire Assembly R.R. - Properly secured, no loose or missing lug nuts; no visible damage.
9. Lift Cylinder Rod End Shaft - Properly secured; evidence of proper lubrication (lubricate every 10 hours).
10. Fuel Supply - Fuel filler cap secure. Tank - no visible damage; no evidence of leaks.
11. Control Valve Compartment - No loose or missing parts; evidence of leakage; unsupported wires or hoses; damaged or broken wires.
12. Hydraulic Oil Supply - Recommended oil level approximately 3 inches from top of sight gauge - gasoline engine; middle of sight gauge - electric machine (check level with cold oil, systems shut down, machine in stowed position). Cap secure and in place. On electric machine, oil tank is located on opposite side of machine.
13. Hydraulic Oil Filter Housing - Housing secure; no visible damage or signs of leakage.
14. Hydraulic Oil Breather - Element in place, not clogged, no signs of overflow.
15. Turntable Springs - Properly secured, no loose or missing nuts or bolts.
16. Steer Wheel/Tire Assembly, Right Front - Properly secured; no loose or missing lug nuts; no visible damage.
17. Extendable Axle - Lock pins in place, properly secured. Check both sides.
18. Ground Controls - Switches operable; no visible damage; placards secure and legible.
19. Tie Rod and Steering Linkage - No loose or missing parts; no visible damage. Tie rod end studs locked.
20. Steer Wheel/Tire Assembly, Left Front - Properly secured; no loose or missing lug nuts; no visible damage.
21. Muffler and Exhaust System - Properly secured; no evidence of leakage.
22. Engine Oil Supply - Full mark on dipstick; filler cap secure.
23. Battery - Proper electrolyte level; cables tight, no visible damage or corrosion.
24. Cowling and Latches - All cowling, doors, and latches in working condition, properly secured, no loose or missing parts.
25. Air Shrouding - No visible damage; loose or missing hardware. No obstructions.
26. Turntable Bearing and Pinion - No loose or missing hardware; visible damage, evidence of proper lubrication. No evidence of loose bolts or looseness between bearing and structure.
27. Engine Air Filter Assembly - No loose or missing parts, no visible damage, element clean.
28. Drive Hub - No visible damage; evidence of leakage.
29. Drive Wheel/Tire Assembly, Left Rear - Properly secured; no loose or missing lug nuts; no visible damage.
30. Frame - No visible damage; loose or missing hardware (top and underside).
31. Boom Sections - No visible damage; wear pads secure; boom chain adjusting nuts secure and undamaged.
32. Powertrack - No loose, damaged or missing parts; hydraulic and electrical lines - no visible damage.
33. Platform Pivot and Slave Cylinder Attach Pins - Properly secured; evidence of proper lubrication (where applicable).
34. Extend-a-Reach Attach Pin - (if equipped) - Properly secured, evidence of proper lubrication (where applicable).

Figure 2-1. Daily Walkaround Inspection.(Sheet 2 of 2)

FROM THE VERTEX 110 PERSONNEL LIFT MANUAL

Base Control Panel

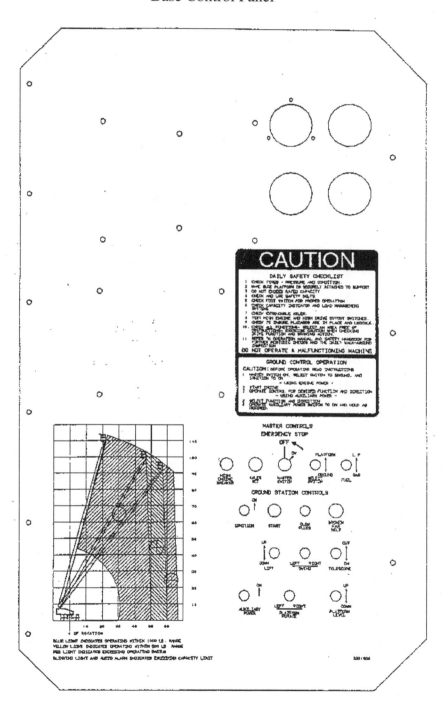

FROM THE VERTEX 110 PERSONNEL LIFT MANUAL
BASKET CONTROL PANEL

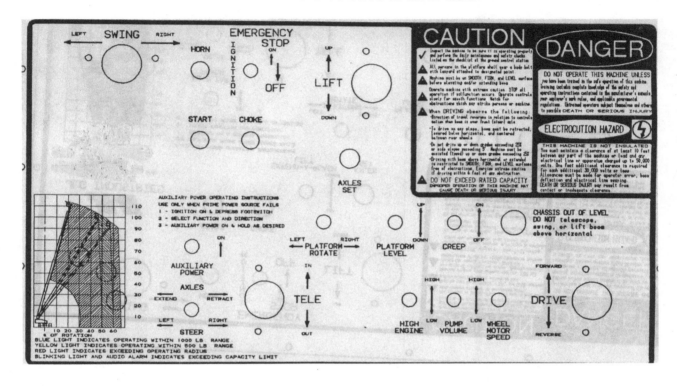

FROM THE VERTEX 110 PERSONNEL LIFT MANUAL
BLOWUP—BASKET CONTROL PANEL LMS

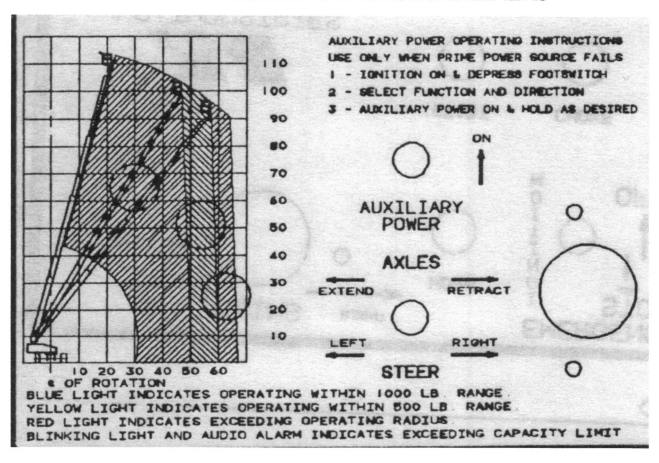

Exhibit 2

Simplified Wiring Diagram

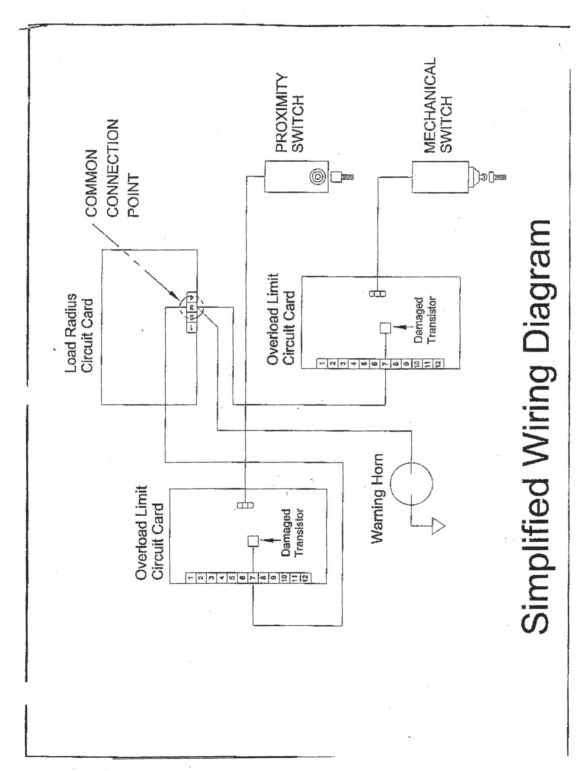

Exhibit 3

Marine Resources Personnel Lift Training and Certification Checklist

Here are the everyday safety precautions that must be obeyed whenever any employee is assigned any work process that requires a personnel lift to be used as a work platform.

• All operators must receive training prior to using a personnel lift.

• Wear a full body harness over land, and a life jacket over water.

• Before starting the lift make sure that there is propane in the lift's bottle; do not use gasoline.

• When changing propane bottles, always screw the fuel line coupling completely down and turn the valve to the "On" position before you start the lift.

• Check engine fluid levels (oil, water, fuel).

• Visually inspect all structural parts for damage, including the tires.

• Start engine, allow engine to warm up.

• If the engine will not start, notify the maintenance crew.

• Know your platform load limits. Most platforms are rated at a 500 pound maximum.

• Never exceed the manufacturer's platform load capacity.

• The load capacity is the combined weight of personnel, tools, and materials.

• Make sure the unit is on firm and level ground.

• Lifts shall never be used as a crane or hoist.

• Do not use the unit if it is not functioning properly.

• The lift must not be used as a welding ground.

• Lifts are noninsulated and must not be operated within 10 feet of a 50,000 volt line.

• Do not lean over platform guardrails to perform work.

• Do not use ladders or scaffolding on the platform to obtain greater height.

• Do not drive carriage or platform into stationary objects.

• Keep objects clear of the foot pedal in the platform.

• Do not alter or override any hydraulic, mechanical, or electrical safety devices on the lift.

• Do not work on the platform if you feel dizzy or unsteady in any way.

• Do not jumpstart other vehicles.

• Only use propane bottles that are labeled "vapor," liquid bottles will freeze the unit.

• If the propane bottle becomes frosty and the engine speed starts to fluctuate, you are running out of propane. Change the bottle. Do not drain the battery!

• When finished using lift, always turn key to the "Off" position to avoid battery drain.

Exhibit 4

VERTEX MANUFACTURING MEMORANDUM

To: Joyce Stewart, VP Manufacturing

CC: Norman Knitpicker, Vertex General Counsel

From: Marvin Felix, Safety Engineering

Date: January 29, YR-1

Subj: 110 Lift Tip-Over at Marine Resources

<><><><><><><><><><><><><><><><><><><><><><><><><><><><><><><><><><><><><>

In early October YR-2, I was informed by Mr. Demsky at Marine Resources Shipyard (MRS) that a 110-foot Vertex personnel lift that MRS had recently bought had tipped over and injured two MRS workers who were in the basket painting the side of a ship. After informing you and our insurance carrier, I received a call from our general counsel who told me that he had arranged for me to inspect the lift at the shipyard.

I inspected the Vertex 110 lift involved in this accident on two occasions, December 12, YR-2, and January 23, YR-1. An independent investigator hired by the shipyard, a Mr. Gerhard, was present during the second inspection.

I have seen Mr. Gerhard's pictures and read his report regarding the condition of the lift immediately after the accident. I agree with his report through his "Initial Conclusion" regarding the post-accident condition and capabilities of the lift, and that the basket had not been overloaded at the time of the fall. However, I disagree with his report from that point on, especially his conclusions regarding why this accident happened as it did and the lack of the circuit cards' redundancy.

During my investigation of the accident, I found that this lift had the original type of LMS circuit cards, that is, not the new design with the automatically resetting fuse. The switches on the lift's Load Management System's (LMS) two circuit boards were not functioning properly due to being damaged, possibly by an electrical overload that burned out a transistor on the cards. This caused the LMS's tip-over warning light and siren and its tip-over prevention mechanism, which locks out the "boom out" and "boom down" functions, to fail.

Notwithstanding the failure of the LMS circuit cards, the LMS's load safety zone indicator lights on the control panels were working. Thus, operating the basket up to fifty feet from the base with the boom extended would cause the green indicator light to illuminate; operating the basket up to sixty feet from the base would cause the yellow light to illuminate; and operating the basket between sixty and seventy feet horizontally would cause the red light to illuminate steadily.

It is clear that the workers in the lift's basket moved the boom and basket into the red light zone and then beyond the safe zone of operation, causing the lift to tip over.

The lift was otherwise operating normally within its limits.

Strong external electrical currents can cause an electrical overload in the LMS and short out a circuit card. It is hard for me to tell exactly what level of electrical currents were present at Marine Resources on the day of the accident, as they were not tested at that time. I have not returned to the MRS shipyard to look for possible overload sources since things had changed on the dock since the accident.

I learned that the workers who fell in the lift did not follow proper safety procedures and did not inspect the LMS before beginning their shift working in the lift. This instruction is written clearly on a yellow decal that is on the turret next to the base control panel. One of the injured workers has stated that prior to the accident they did not come into contact with any known strong source of electrical current that could have overloaded the LMS circuit cards.

Therefore, while what caused the LMS circuit boards to short out is still unknown, it is my conclusion that the failure of the circuit cards occurred before the injured workers began their shift, and that the accident was caused by the failure of the workers to test the equipment. Had they followed correct procedures, they would have discovered the electrical fault in the LMS and avoided this accident.

I have cc'd our General Counsel on this report just in case there is some litigation arising from this matter.

Exhibit 5

Vertex Industries, Inc.
5800 Brassfield Road
Raleigh, NC 27614

September 27, YR-5

Mr. Leland Motley
Project Manager
Schultz Consolidated
Hoboken, NJ 07030

Re: August 26, YR-5 Accident at Schultz Plant in Hoboken, New Jersey

Dear Mr. Motley:

This letter is in response to your September letter whereby you requested that we advise you of the results of our investigation of the Vertex Model 110 personnel lift involved in the subject accident.

As you know, following notification of this accident, we arrived the morning after to inspect and test the machine. At that time, we determined that the controls were functioning properly. The capacity indicator/radius chart lights were functional, but the audio alarm was not. We also determined that neither of the load management system circuits was working. All of the warning decals were in place and legible.

On September 8, we sent an engineer and a technician to the repairing dealer to troubleshoot the load management system. They found that the circuit cards for both the proximity switch and the mechanical switch were not functioning correctly. Replacing one circuit card restored the load management system's function; replacing the second card restored its redundancy. The audio alarm was found to have an open circuit. Further, the alarm was wired with the polarity reversed. This may have caused the short circuit that led to damage to the circuit cards. Correctly installing a new alarm restored total function.

As you may be aware, the load management system on the Vertex 110 is supposed to be checked before each day's operation. Warnings and instructions are located at the ground control panel. Each of the items found would have been detected during the required daily check. The four items found could not have occurred simultaneously.

The tip-over occurred because the operator did not adhere to the capacity lights and moved the machine into an unstable configuration and because the machine and its safety systems were not properly inspected prior to use.

Of course, we are greatly concerned about your injured equipment operators and hope they have fully recovered and returned to work. If the Vertex Model 110 is checked, maintained, and operated in accordance with the product warnings and manuals, your operators should have no fear for their personal safety.

Sincerely,

VERTEX INDUSTRIES, INC.

Marvin Felix

Marvin Felix
Director-Product Safety & Reliability

MF

Exhibit 6

PRECISION FAILURE ANALYSIS
CONFIDENTIAL REPORT

October 22, YR-2

Ms. Olivia Morris, General Counsel
Marine Resources Shipyard, Inc.
P.O. Box 1991
Nita City, Nita 55505

Re: Analysis of Personnel Lift Tip-Over Accident on October 2, YR-2

Dear Ms. Morris:

On October 2, YR-2, your company requested that Precision Failure Analysis (PFA) analyze a tip-over accident of a personnel lift, which occurred at Marine Resources Shipyard (Marine Resources) in Nita City that same day. The accident occurred without any apparent warning and two men were seriously injured. I reported to your shipyard the next morning, October 3, and investigated the accident and the lift.

Background
Marine Resources employee Melvin Demsky reported that workers Raymond Garcia and John Machado were painting the outer hall of the dry-docked cruise ship Smorgasbord at approximately 4:35 p.m. on October 2, YR-2, when the personnel lift that they were riding in tipped over, throwing both men to the ground. Both men were hospitalized. The accident occurred at the beginning of the swing shift. Weather was overcast, the dock was dry, and visibility was approximately 1,000 feet at ground level. Machado reported that the machine tipped over suddenly without warning. No alarm was heard by any shipyard personnel.

Analysis
Multiple interviews with personnel from Marine Resources were the primary source of information for this analysis. Several pieces of documentation were also reviewed, provided by the same personnel.

A.   Description of the Equipment.
The personnel lift involved in the accident was 110-foot boom, two-wheel drive, self-propelled unit, identified as a Vertex Model 110. It was purchased by Marine Resources directly from Vertex approximately four weeks earlier. It was typically operated by numerous shipyard personnel throughout the work week. It was a universal piece of equipment, often used for paint and welding operations, or any other general above-ground tasks. The long reach of the unit was achieved by four telescoping box beam

sections, referred to as the base, the inner mid-section, the outer mid-section, and the fly section, which supports the basket.

The unit is hydraulically operated by joystick controls in the basket. Secondary controls were behind the access cover on the back of the turret. The unit was heavily marked with safety warnings on numerous locations, including both control consoles. An area of primary safety focus is the three-color diagram on each console illustrating what is known as the "safety zone."

In general, the lift can support the heaviest loads possible with the load over the base. For an extended boom, this requires that the boom be near vertical. Safely raising a heavy basket load requires that the boom be elevated ("angled") prior to being extended ("telescoped out"). Safe lowering requires the reverse, thus maintaining the load as nearly over the base as possible. A heavy basket load extended horizontally beyond the safe range from the base imperils the unit. The result tip-over is endemic to any boomed lifting device, such as cranes or personnel lifts.

B.   Weight in the Basket.

In typical fashion for personnel lifts, the manufacturer gave the machine a dual weight rating or limit. It was rated at 1,000 pounds mass (lbm.) if the load is within 50 horizontal feet of the center line of the turret, then it was rated to 500 lbm. for loads between 50 and 60 horizontal feet from the turret. For simplicity and safety, the machine had a single basket load rating of 500 lbm. imposed by Marine Resources. This is consistent with all other personnel lift weight ratings at Marine Resources.

The combined weight of the two men and their equipment at the time of the accident was estimated to be 476 lbm. This is based upon the following personnel and material in the basket:

a.   Mr. Garcia, 186 lbm.

b.   Mr. Machado, 210 lbm.

c.   One-half bucket blue paint, 25 lbm.

d.   Two power rollers, 10 lbm.

e.   Two paint lines, 25 lbm.

f.   Clothing for men, 20 lbm.

       Total: 476 lbm.

The total calculated was within the 500 lbm. weight limit in effect. No basket overload situation is likely in this incident. Nor was it considered a possibility by any of the individuals interviewed for this report.

Operation

Due to the great amount of tipping force ("leverage") produced, the long boom length requires relatively little weight to upset even a very heavy base. The weight of the Vertex Model 110 is 35,000 lbm., yet it is still easily upset by over-extension of its boom.

This is why a "load management system" is incorporated in the design of this product. It limits movement of the boom's angle and extension to accommodations only allowed within the safety zone. Normal operation is within the blue area shown on the control panel. In this area, the machine is highly stable and is actually rated by the manufacturer for 1,000 lbm. in the basket. When being operated in this zone, a blue light is lit on the control panel. Less stable conditions of angle and extension move the machine into the yellow or caution zone, which also turns off the blue light and turns on the yellow light. The manufacturer sets a load limit for the basket of 500 lbm. in this region. Further extension or downward movement of the boom causes the yellow light to go off and the red light to go on, indicating that the machine is dangerously close to tipping. At this point the basket is within the last 25 percent of safe operation without tipping over. Further extension or lowering of the boom causes the red light to blink, and an audio alarm to sound. At this point, the machine automatically locks out further boom extension or downward rotation. Only safe combinations of basket movement, that is, either up or in, are possible. Doing this will bring the unit back to a condition of stability and stop the red light from blinking and silence the alarm.

Due to its extremely long reach of 110 feet, this particular unit is more prone to tipping over than other models observed. Testing at the accident scene verified that it was incapable of lifting its own fully extended boom off the ground even with no load in the basket. Attempts to do so resulted in the base tipping over. On the subject of typical personnel lift stability, PFA interviewed Melvin Demsky of Marine Resources, who is highly experienced with personnel lifts. He had no prior experience with a personnel lift like this that could tip itself over in an unloaded condition solely by attempting to raise the fully extended boom off the ground.

During the discussion, another Vertex unit was examined at Marine Resources. It was marked 36,000 lbm., similar to the unit involved in the accident, yet was only capable of the 60 foot boom extension. Due to its shorter reach, the smaller unit was an inherently more stable machine than the unit involved in the accident, and was demonstrated by Mr. Demsky to be able to lift its fully extended boom off the ground even with Mr. Demsky in its basket. The demonstration on the smaller unit was conducted without any machine alarm being set off, and no automatic limitation of the operator's control inputs was observed.

Condition of the Personnel Lift

The personnel lift involved in the accident was inspected at the accident scene by PFA between the mornings of October 3 and October 4, YR-2. It was found to have its boom extended 86.4 feet, measured from center of the boom pivot pin to the center of the basket pin. Photographs were taken by Marine Resources personnel prior to any disturbance of the machine's position. That night the front wheels were then let down to the ground based on safety concerns. The boom was sagging in its center sections due to buckling damage from the impact. The basket was severely distorted due primarily to the high impact forces generated by the weights of the two men. The level deck of the dry-dock was indented approximately 3/8 of an inch due to the impact of the basket and of the boom on the deck.

The combination of boom elevation and extension was clearly beyond the normal safe operational range of the machine. The boom struck the deck, causing its apparent elevation angle to be increased. This indicated that, if anything, the boom angle was actually closer to horizontal immediately prior to impact than was measured after the accident. The result would have been an even more unstable position than just calculated.

The amount to which the boom was extended was not in question since the accident had damaged it in such a way as to prevent any of the sections from telescoping into each other. This is also consistent with descriptions by numerous personnel of Marine Resources.

According to the safety zone diagrams provided on the machine's basket, on its turret, and in the service manuals, the boom and basket were clearly beyond the safe zone of operation and the following three events should have been in progress:

1. The boom should not be able to be lowered.

2. The red lights should be flashing on both the basket and on the turret.

3. The alarm should be sounding.

It should be noted that the lift was reported to have been working properly for the entire shift immediately proceeding the accident.

Attempt to Raise the Boom

Further evaluation involved attempting to raise the boom while at the 86.4 foot extension of the accident. The engine was started and the hydraulic controls were found to be operating smoothly and relatively normally, with three important exceptions:

1. The angle control of the boom could not be operated in a manner that would raise or lower the boom's angle.

2. The red light was steadily on instead of flashing.

3. The alarm did not sound.

Conclusions

Based on the proceeding analysis and the information available at the time, we conclude the following:

1. The personnel lift in this accident is significantly less stable than the models that the experienced personnel at Marine Resources are accustomed to.

2. The personnel lift was not being misused at the time of the accident.

3. The personnel lift was not overloaded at the time of the accident.

4. The boom of the personnel lift was somehow allowed by the machine's load management control system to reach significantly beyond the machine's safe working envelope, strongly suggesting a major load management system malfunction.

5. The alarm and flasher in the load management system of the personnel lift was not functioning properly at the time of the accident, again strongly suggesting a control malfunction.

Thank you for using Precision Failure Analysis. If you have any questions, or we can be of further assistance to you, please do not hesitate to contact us.

Sincerely,

Werner Gerhard

WERNER GERHARD, PE
Senior Project Manager

WG

Exhibit 7

MARINE RESOURCES DOCK AFTER TIP-OVER (1)

Exhibit 8

MARINE RESOURCES DOCK AFTER TIP-OVER (2)

Exhibit 9

PERSONNEL LIFT CONTROL PANEL

Exhibit 10

SAFETY DECAL—PROCEDURE FOR DAILY CHECK OF LOAD MANAGEMENT SYSTEM ON LIFT TURRET

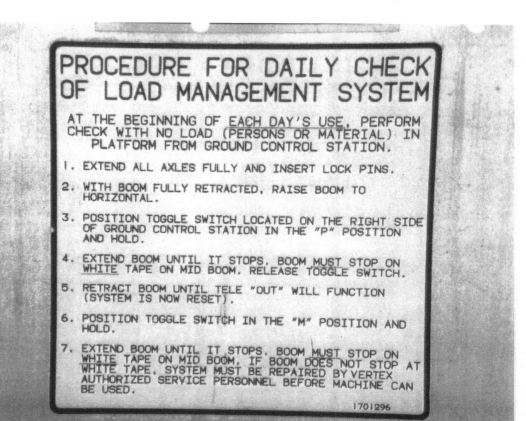

Exhibit 11

Decal—Daily Safety Checklist on Ground Control Panel

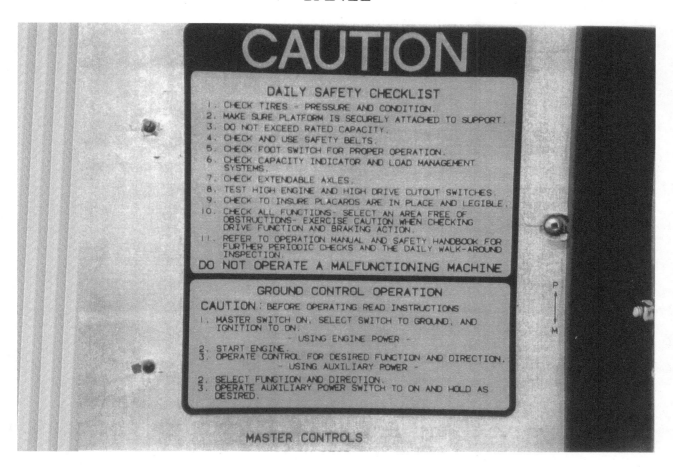

Exhibit 12

LIFT'S LMS CIRCUIT CARDS—LOAD MANAGEMENT SYSTEM

M Card

P Card

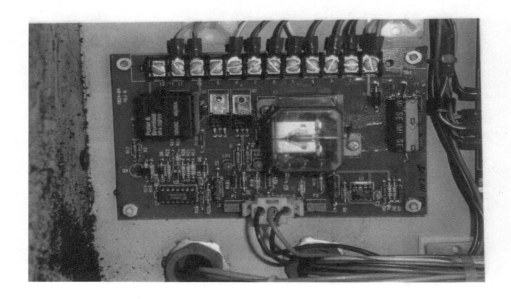

Exhibit 13

CIRCUIT CARD WITHOUT RESETTING FUSE

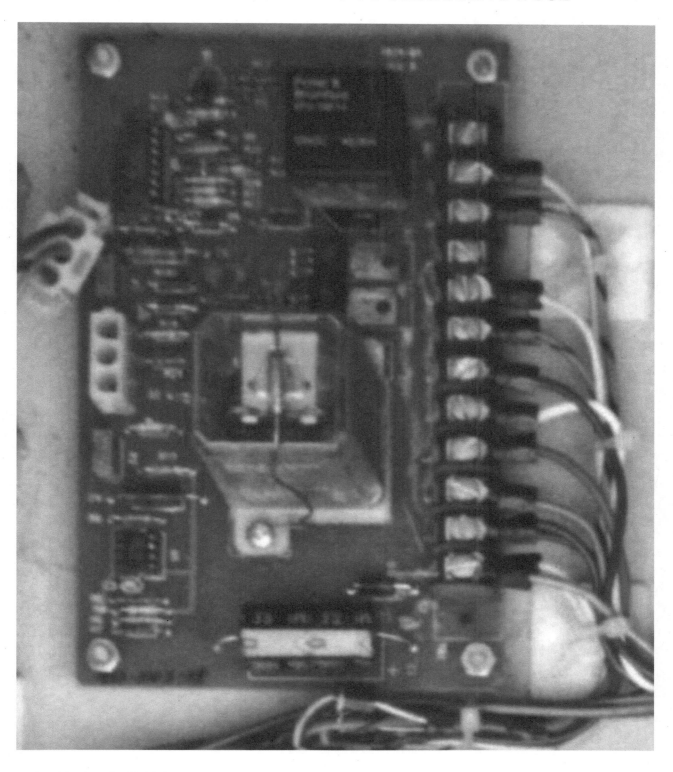

Exhibit 14

CIRCUIT CARD WITH RESETTING FUSE

Exhibit 15

New and Old Circuit Cards Side by Side

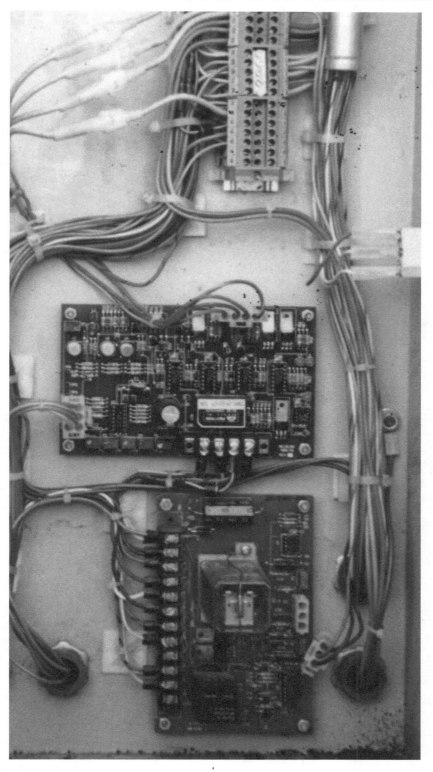

Basket Control Panel Model Close-Up

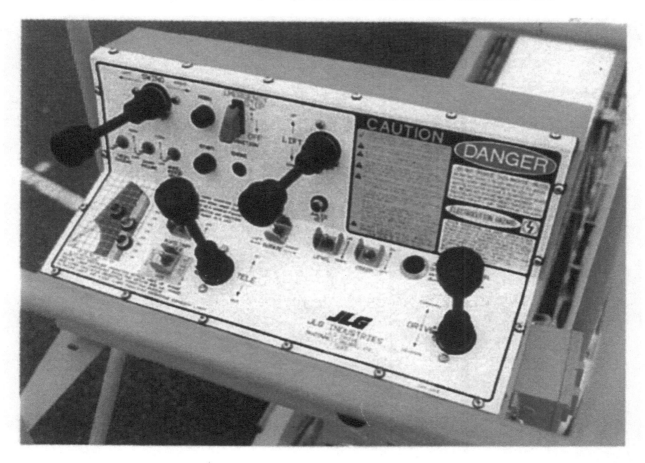

Complete machine operation is provided from the platform control station which includes the load management indicator system.

Exhibit 17

Basket Control Panel—Right Side

Exhibit 18

BASKET CONTROL PANEL—WARNINGS CLOSE-UP

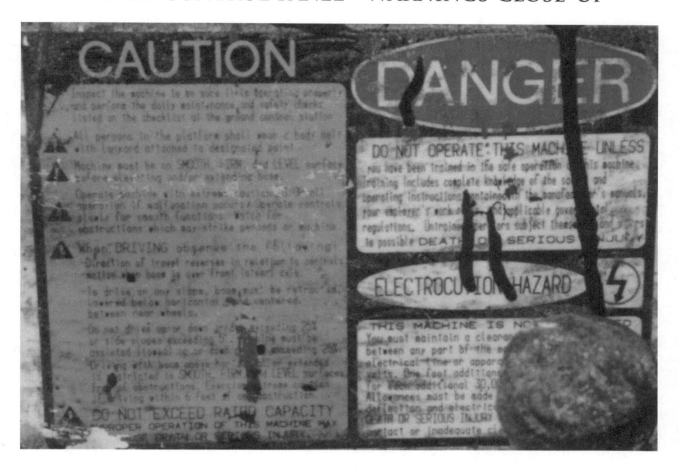

Exhibit 19

Basket Control Panel—Caution/Danger Decal

Exhibit 20a

COMPUTER GRAPHIC OF LIFT FALL

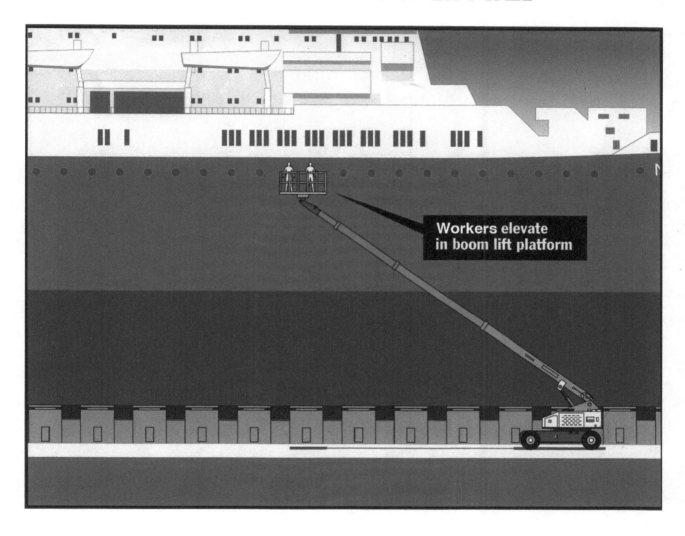

Workers elevate
in boom lift platform

COMPUTER GRAPHIC OF LIFT FALL

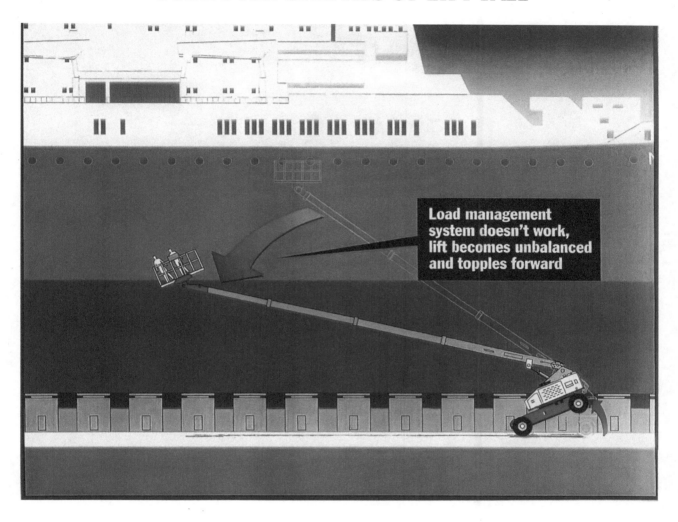

Load management system doesn't work, lift becomes unbalanced and topples forward

COMPUTER GRAPHIC OF LIFT FALL

DEPOSITION OF STELLA GARCIA
MAY 14, YR-1

1   My name is Stella Garcia. I am fifty-eight years old. I am currently employed as a guidance
2   counselor in the Nita School District. Before that, I worked for the Darrow County Sheriff's
3   Department as a secretary/receptionist.

4   My second son, Ray, was born on Mother's Day, May 12, YR-36. He was a joy to me. From the
5   day he came home from the hospital, he responded to everyone. His interpersonal strengths were
6   present even then. He smiled early and often, with a snuggly, cuddly nature.

7   When Ray and his eldest brother were youngsters, I stayed home and cared for them. Their
8   father and I divorced when Ray was only three. He was a police officer. After our divorce, he moved
9   to Keetonville to find a job as a cop there. He usually visited Ray and his brother only around
10 Christmas. When I was on my own, I operated a childcare center out of our home. It did not take
11 Ray very long, as young as he was, to start making friends with all the other children. He always
12 shared his toys and had a natural ability to understand others. He had many friends. He has very
13 strong cooperative skills. Ray has always been a team player and continued that same winning at-
14 titude until October 2, YR-2. Up to that day, Ray was a happy boy with sparkling eyes and that
15 ever-present smile that lit up his face.

16 Ray was never involved in conflict. He had a loving, cooperative nature, with strong problem
17 solving skills. I know he was arrested and got probation for fighting with his girlfriend, Annie Rose.
18 But I know Ray would not attack her. She came at him and he defended himself. However, these
19 days it is always the man's fault. Ray's father complained often that the law required them to charge
20 the men and never the women in any domestic fight. It is not fair. However, Ray and Annie are
21 getting alone fine. They live together with her son. I'm over there quite often to help look after her
22 son and to visit Ray. Annie is on unemployment and gets child welfare benefits, but she is going to
23 school now.

24 He showed responsibility and worked early on. He had a paper route for many years. He knew
25 everyone on his route and spent time visiting with his customers. He received gifts on holidays and
26 always gave good service.

27 Ray never liked school. He did best in classes where he had hands-on experiences and could
28 apply his knowledge in practical situations. Rote memorization, learning facts and regurgitating
29 them on standard paper and pencil tests, was not one of his strengths. He did not have as many
30 opportunities in school to display his intelligence as students do today. We are just finding out now
31 about the different ways children learn. Ray has a much more creative bent than most, which is not
32 easily measured on rote memory tests. Today he would be rewarded academically for his abilities.

1   We just did not know how to measure them in the past. Ray was not a discipline problem in school

2   and cooperated with his teachers.

3   However, his teachers would always complain to me at parent-teachers meetings and through

4   notes that Ray sometimes "spaced out" in class and was not paying attention. A couple of teachers

5   said they had difficulty getting Ray's attention even when they called on him. However, Ray was just

6   a daydreamer. Sometimes when he was supposed to be doing his homework, I'd find him staring out

7   the window, a world away. He never "spaced out" like he was in a trance or having a "fit."

8   Ray has hay fever. As a child, he'd get terrible sore throats—tonsillitis. When Ray was five or

9   six, he came down with a serious throat infection and had a dangerously high temperature, 105 or

10 106. At one point, he seemed to go into a state of semi-consciousness—he wouldn't respond when

11 I spoke to him, but he seemed awake. I took him to the hospital ER. They gave him shots and kept

12 him overnight. His doctor told me that Ray wouldn't have any permanent effects from the high

13 fever. After his high fever, his tonsils were removed, and he never had another high fever.

14   Ray has many lifelong friends. He gets along well with all people and shows great compassion.

15 He was able to use his love of people and is great interpersonal skills in real estate. By the time of his

16 accident, he had gotten his real estate license and was dabbling in real estate on the side. One year

17 he made around $40,000 from it. He was amazing. He never gave up, persevering in getting listings,

18 finding buyers, and taking care of the needs of everyone involved in a transaction. He always saw

19 obstacles as challenges. Any problem could be solved.

20   All of that ended on October 2, YR-2. When I got to Memorial Hospital, Ray was unconscious.

21 He was gray and bloody. Exhibit 26 is a picture of one of his head wounds. He had another on the

22 back of his head. He had no memory of the accident. When he finally roused to consciousness, we

23 had to close the drapes because he had developed an acute sensitivity to light.

24   Since the accident, from the first days in the hospital to now, he has panic attacks. He has a

25 tremendous fear of heights. He is unable to continue working at the shipyard.

26   The son that I knew and loved so much has ceased to exist. The bright smile and sparkling eyes

27 that lit up his face are gone. My hardworking, independent son is now a dependent, emotional

28 cripple who cannot handle the basics of everyday living. Little problems become catastrophes that

29 he dwells on endlessly, repeating the same information over and over again.

30   He is very discouraged and distressed. Not only is the constant pain with him, along with fear,

31 but he is so frustrated that he can do so little. He has terrible nightmares. His powers of concen-

32 tration are limited. He cannot handle more than one simple task at a time. He stresses on simple

33 things, so much so that they become an obsession.

34   Ray's reading ability is adversely affected. He cannot focus his eyes on small print. He cannot

35 read large chunks of information without becoming confused. As a result, he can't continue devel-

36 oping his real estate career.

1   I am his mother. I know him like no other person in the world. I am convinced that he has

2   been having seizure activity in his brain since the accident on October 2. Every once and awhile,

3   he'll seem to go into a trance. I speak to him, but he doesn't respond. He comes out of it after ten or

4   fifteen seconds, but he doesn't remember my speaking to him. Ray's girl friend, Annie, told me that

5   she has noticed Ray "spacing out" occasionally since the accident. Dr. Moretti's brain test shows that

6   I am right. As long as there is a breath of life in me, I will not stop working to help my son get what

7   he deserves. He needs care, and somebody needs to accept responsibility and ought to pay for it.

This deposition was taken in the office of defendant's counsel on May 14, YR-1. This deposition was given under oath and was read and signed by the deponent.

Certified by:

Penelope Harrison

_____

Penelope Harrison
Certified Shorthand Reporter
(CSR)

DEPOSITION OF ELENA MORETTI, MD
MAY 29, YR-1

1   My name is Dr. Elena Moretti. I am a neurologist on the staff of Memorial Hospital. I went

2   to the University of Chicago as an undergraduate and then graduated from University of Virginia

3   Medical School. I did my internship and residency at San Francisco General Hospital. Since that

4   time, I have been Associate Professor at the Department of Neurological Surgery at University of

5   Nita, as well as the Director of the Regional Epilepsy Center at Memorial Hospital.

6   I was asked to see Raymond Garcia by one of his attending physicians at Memorial Hospital

7   following his industrial accident of October 2, YR-2. He had been placed on a prophylactic course

8   of Dilantin.

9   My initial consultation note indicates that he was injured on October 2, YR-2, at Marine

10   Resources Shipyard when a crane he was in fell seventy feet. He broke both ankles, recoiled in bas-

11   ket and hit his head. He doesn't recall the accident. He was told that he spoke gibberish, tore off his

12   clothing, tried to run, and exhibited confused behavior. His first memory following the accident

13   was while being treated in the trauma center at Memorial Hospital.

14   Mr. Garcia told me that since the industrial accident, among other problems, he has had several

15   different kinds of "spells," characterized by staring blankly or spacing out. It was the view of the

16   referring neurologist that this represented a potential seizure disorder. My notes indicate that in ad-

17   dition to these seizures, he has some retrograde amnesia for the week prior to the injury.

18   I have never been involved in a court case before. I didn't know that this was going to turn into

19   a legal matter, so my focus wasn't really on trying to establish any legal story. I was just trying to

20   take care of him. I decided to work with patients with seizure disorders because I felt this was an

21   excellent way for me to make a difference, to use my skills to help people who faced these enormous

22   medical challenges in life.

23   The records are a bit unclear on whether Mr. Garcia was in a frank coma following the accident

24   of October 2, YR-2. He was responsive to stimuli. He was in a great deal of pain initially.

25   I concluded that his head injury was moderately severe from a clinical standpoint. There is a

26   broad range of possibilities here. You can have anywhere from a little concussion of the brain stem,

27   or a full attention deficit disorder, to encephalomalacia or where you actually have a bleed into the

28   brain. There is a broad range of severity. In any event, I do not think that Mr. Garcia's head injury

29   was merely mild. The combination of having lost consciousness, being amnesic to the event, his

30   coworker's description of how he jumped up and had unusual behavior—tore off his clothes, was

31   speaking gibberish, and ran around in a confused manner—and the location and severity of the

32   head injury, all suggest to me that he had a fairly significant head injury.

1   Many times we see people who have sustained trauma acting in a very volatile manner for
2   periods of time. His unusual behavior struck me as being an indication of at least a moderately
3   severe injury. It really does not matter to me that he may have been unconscious for only several
4   minutes.

5   I disagree with Dr. Coffin's opinion that the length of time a patient is unconscious always de-
6   termines the severity of the head injury, particularly in a case like this, where there is no question
7   that Mr. Garcia received a serious blow to the head. Just as a matter of elementary physics and grav-
8   ity, there was an enormous energy transfer to Mr. Garcia's head and body in the sudden stop that
9   followed the seventy foot fall.

10   There was a vague suggestion in one of Mr. Garcia's medical records that he may have had pos-
11   sible petit mal seizures as a child. There is no indication whether an actual diagnosis was ever made,
12   and if so, whether it was on the basis of an EEG or something else. There is no support from any
13   family member for the proposition that this childhood issue was particularly significant. When he
14   was five or six years old, he ran a high fever at one point, became limp and started to shake. His
15   mother reports that they rushed him to the doctor, who said that this was just a reaction to the fe-
16   ver, calling it a febrile seizure. His mother states that after he had his tonsils out, there was no more
17   problem with temperature or febrile seizures.

18   I disagree with Dr. Coffin that this patient is an unreliable historian. The medical events of
19   early childhood often are not well encoded in the brain. There was no suggestion that Mr. Garcia
20   was withholding information or trying to make up a story here to support causation. He is genu-
21   inely concerned about what his symptoms following this accident will mean for his future. And his
22   mother was able to provide sufficient details for me to conclude that there was no support for any
23   diagnosis of a preexisting seizure disorder, as Dr. Coffin tries to suggest.

24   Unlike Dr. Coffin, who did no clinical studies of her own, I performed a twenty-four-hour
25   EEG CC/TV monitored study at Memorial Hospital. This was done on October 3, YR-2, after the
26   administration of chlorohydrate. It was interpreted as abnormal, consistent with a trauma induced
27   seizure disorder. During brief wakefulness and mainly drowsiness, epileptiform patterns were mani-
28   fest over the left inferior frontal-mid temporal scalp regions. A focal non-epileptiform disturbance
29   was also observed over left frontal-temporal scalp regions. Exhibit 23 is the test printout. I circled
30   the epileptiform pattern on the printout.

31   Based on the history, my examinations, and the EEG study, I conclude that Mr. Garcia sus-
32   tained a seizure disorder in the tip-over accident at Marine Resources Shipyard. Dr. Coffin's conclu-
33   sion to the contrary fails to explain the onset of this patient's symptoms following this documented
34   head trauma. I see no evidence either of malingering or conversion reaction.

1   Based on the causal relationship between the industrial accident and the seizure disorder that I
2   have diagnosed in this patient, he will require medical care for the remainder of his life. This can be
3   broken down into the following categories:

4   1. Neurologist-yearly follow-up examinations. $200–$240 each time, once per year. Average
5   annual cost—$220.

6   2. Electroencephalography (EEG) yearly, to record and monitor electrical activity of the
7   brain, looking for any signs of worsening or progression. $731 each time, once per year. Annual
8   cost—$731.

9   3. Anti-seizure medication (e.g., Depakote, 125 mg). $66.76 per month. Annual
10   cost—$801.12

11   4. Complete blood count (CBC) yearly, to check for medication side effects. Annual
12   cost—$36.

13   5. Renal function panel (RFP) yearly, to assess medication effects on the liver. Annual
14   cost—$41.

15   Typically, the patient would have his EEG, CBC, and RFP completed each year. Those results
16   would go to the neurologist for review for the annual follow-up appointment. If there is no increase
17   in symptoms in the period of time between visits, then the patient would return the following year
18   for a repeat examination.

19   The total annual cost of Mr. Garcia's follow-up care necessitated by this industrial accident is
20   $1,829.12. Assuming a fifty year life expectancy, the total cost of this would be $91,456.00. This is
21   quite a conservative projection, not taking into account the almost certain rise in the cost of these
22   services in the future. It also does not factor in the much greater expense if scar tissue in the brain
23   due to this trauma builds up even more, causing a worsening of the seizure disorder. In such a case,
24   the costs of medical care and monitoring can be expected to go up dramatically.

25   For an industrial worker such as Mr. Garcia, the worsening of his seizure disorder would have a
26   very significant impact on his ability to earn a living, due to the greater risk of falls and injury. The
27   worsening of his seizure disorder could also mean disqualification from driving a car or operating
28   equipment.

This deposition was taken in the office of defendant's counsel on May 29, YR-1. This deposition was given under oath, and was read and signed by the deponent.

Certified by:

Penelope Harrison

Penelope Harrison
Certified Shorthand Reporter
(CSR)

Exhibit 21

MEMORIAL HOSPITAL ADMISSION NOTE

Date & Hour: 10/2/YR-2, 1930 Hours

Patient's Name: Raymond Garcia

Patient admitted secondary to fall from cherry picker at work site. Alert and oriented to name only. Unable to tell place, date, what had happened. Abdomen flat with good bowel tones. Foley catheter patent with clear yellow urine. Admit orders issued. Dressing to head laceration. Both ankles closed fractures. Continued to try to re-orient patient frequently. Family members present. Patient says he hurts "all over." Gradually has become more oriented, now says "I'm in the hospital because I had an accident at work."

Do not suspect any spinal cord injury. Intact sensation. Able to wiggle toes.

Oxycodone given. States it makes him "sick."

Constance McGough

Constance McGough, MD

Exhibit 22

TRANSCRIPT/GRADE RECORD
NITA COMMUNITY COLLEGE

Student Name: Raymond Garcia

SUMMER YR-8

COURSE TITLE	GRADE	CREDIT HOURS
Grammar & Usage	D	5.0
Regional History	C	5.0
Mathematics Clinic	F	5.0

SPRING YR-7

COURSE TITLE	GRADE	CREDIT HOURS
History—The 50s & 60s	C	3.0
Mathematics	B	3.0

FALL YR-7

COURSE TITLE	GRADE	CREDIT HOURS
English Literature	D	3.0
Reading Improvement	Pass	3.0
Fundamentals of Written Communication	B	3.0
Real Estate Principles and Practices	B	3.0

SPRING YR-6

COURSE TITLE	GRADE	CREDIT HOURS
Intro to Business Marketing	B	3.0
Real Estate Finance	B	3.0
Basic Speech/Communication	B	3.0

Exhibit 23

EEG Test Printout

Raymond Garcia

October 3, YR-2

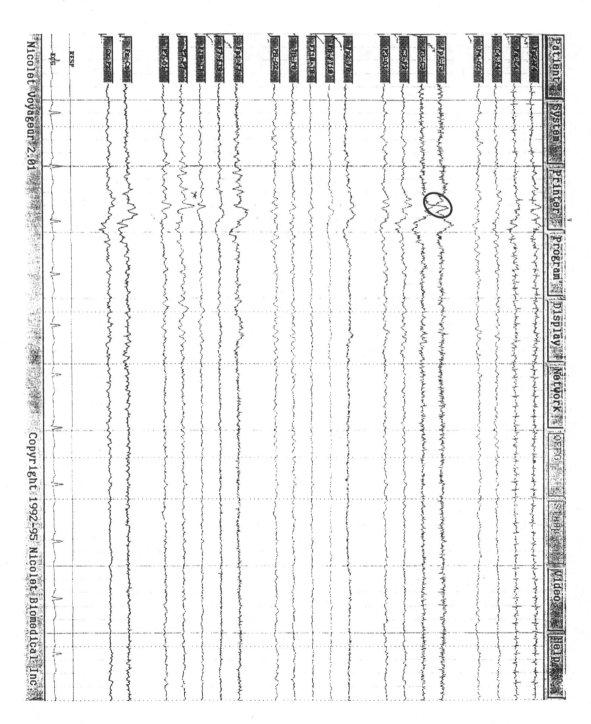

Exhibit 24

MEDICAL REPORT

Physician:	E. Moretti
Location:	Memorial Hospital, Epilepsy Center
Patient's Name:	Raymond Garcia
Age:	34
Sex:	M
Date:	10/3/YR-2

Type of Recording: Sleep, EEG after the oral administration of chlorohydrate.

Findings: This record demonstrates at the outset, patterns of wakefulness and drowsiness. A preponderance of theta and delta range arrhythmic patterns was observed over the left fronto-temporal scalp regions. Sharp waves were observed over left inferior frontal-midtemporal scalp regions (F7-T7). Deeper stages of sleep were not seen.

Interpretation: This record demonstrates during brief wakefulness and mainly drowsiness, epileptiform patterns over left inferior frontal-midtemporal scalp regions. A focal non-epileptiform disturbance was also observed over left fronto-temporal scalp regions.

Elena G. Moretti

Elena G. Moretti, MD
Director, Epilepsy Center

Exhibit 25

REPORTED EARNINGS—RAYMOND GARCIA

YEAR	TOTAL S.S. EARNINGS	REAL ESTATE EARNINGS	TOTAL
YR-12	5,012.99		5,012.99
YR-11	6,557.20		6,557.20
YR-10	8,277.21		8,277.21
YR-9	8,959.95		8,959.95
YR-8	22,431.46		22,431.46
YR-7	2,647.84		2,647.84
YR-6	292.70		292.70
YR-5	408.86	6,674.25	7,083.11
YR-4	3,352.17	38,500.90	41,853.07
YR-3	27,158.08	4,775.00	31,933.08
YR-2	14,380.00	3,547.01	17,927.01

Exhibit 26

Photograph of Ray Garcia's Scalp Laceration

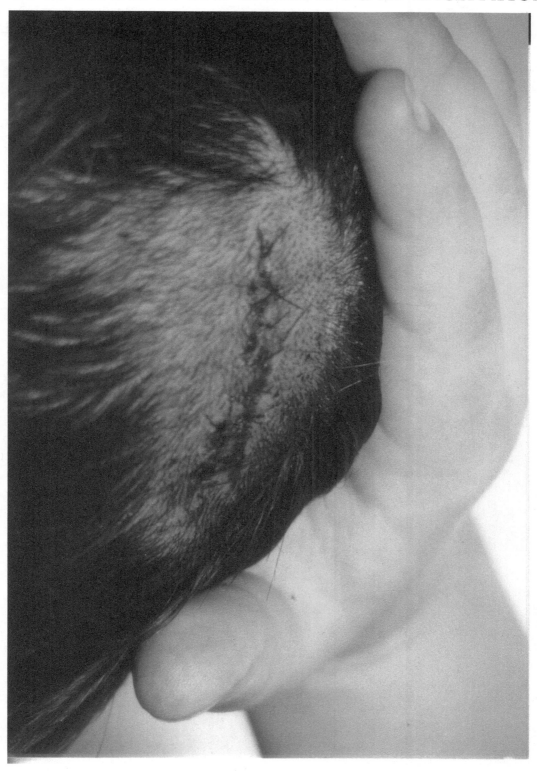

Exhibit 27

MARINE RESOURCES SHIPYARD
EMPLOYEE UNSATISFACTORY PERFORMANCE REPORT

Name: Raymond Garcia

Department: Composite Crew

Badge No.:   7265

Occupation Code: 19

Date: 8/21/YR-2

Shift: First

VIOLATION OF RULES AND REGULATIONS

Rule 2.0 – Attendance. Excessive absenteeism.

REMARKS

Mr. Garcia has had six or more occurrences in the past six (6) months.

WARNING

1st   X_____

2nd   X_____

3rd   X_____

SUPERVISOR'S REVIEW AND RECOMMENDATION

Mr. Garcia is on sixty (60) day probation. Any further policy violations within this period will result in a three (3) day suspension without pay.

Raymond Garcia

EMPLOYEE'S SIGNATURE

(Denotes knowledge of report)

Al Easthouse, Foreman, Composite Crew

Supervisor's Signature & Title

J. MARLENE COFFIN, MD
Clinical Neurologist
1526 Spring Drive, Suite 200
Nita City, Nita 00124

June 4, YR-1

Ms. Eileen Gilbert
Gilbert, Fosnot & Boss
Row Truck Building, Suite 2300
Nita City, Nita 00124

    Re: Raymond Garcia

    Date of Examination: June 4, YR-1

Dear Ms. Gilbert:

At your request, I examined the above-referenced thirty-five-year-old male on June 4, YR-1. As you know, the patient was in an industrial accident on October 2, YR-2, when the personnel lift in which he was riding tipped over at Marine Resources Shipyard. The patient struck his head and sustained bilateral orthopedic injuries. Since that time, an issue has been raised as to whether this patient sustained a seizure disorder. I have reviewed all the records of his prior care that you have furnished me with prior to preparing this report.

CHIEF COMPLAINT

The patient complains of a spacing out feeling, as well as some left-sided neck pain and headaches. He has a feeling of daydreaming as well.

HISTORY OF PRESENT ILLNESS

Mr. Garcia is a fortunate survivor of a seventy foot fall while working at Marine Resources. He does not recall the injury as he has amnesia for the event. He first recalls awakening at Memorial Hospital while he was being treated in the trauma center. He does not recall any diagnosis of a head injury at that time. He has had difficulty sleeping since because of intermittent orthopedic pain. He has noted spacing out episodes in which he dreams and feels he may have lost some time without being aware of it. He also feels restless at times. He has been complaining of tinnitus in his left ear.

NEUROLOGIC REVIEW OF SYSTEMS OTHERWISE IS NEGATIVE

A. Past Medical History.

Past medical history includes that this patient suffered as a child from very high fevers as a result of chronic tonsillitis. During one of these infections when he was five or six years old, he appeared to suffer a seizure of some sort and was hospitalized. My clinical impression is that this patient is not the best historian. When I asked whether he had ever been treated with dilantin as a child, he responded, "I don't think so, but I don't know for sure." However, he states that he has not had any significant prior head injuries, loss of consciousness, seizures, or mental status or cognitive abnormalities prior to this industrial injury.

B. Neurologic Examination.

Neurologic examination shows a normal speech pattern. Cranial nerves are normal. Motor examination is normal throughout. Sensory examination is normal to all modalities tested. Reflexes are present and symmetrical.

DIAGNOSTIC IMPRESSIONS

I do not believe that this patient is suffering from any seizure disorder. While trauma to the brain of the type he sustained can cause the formation of scar tissue, this varies widely from one patient to the next. There is nothing to suggest that this has in fact occurred in this case.

I have reviewed the EEG studies from Memorial Hospital. While there are epileptiform spikes, which are abnormal, these are not positive proof of an actual seizure disorder. They are merely consistent with epileptic potential. Further, the EEG results are not helpful on the causation question in this case. An EEG just confirms what is there, shedding no light on how long it has been there, or what caused the abnormality in the first place.

Based on my training, experience, review of the records and neurological examination results, the most plausible explanation of Mr. Garcia's abnormal EEG is as a dormant artifact of childhood epilepsy that never blossomed into an actual seizure disorder. It does not present any functional problems for this patient in his daily life.

It is very difficult, based on just a patient's history, to determine, first, whether the patient is having real seizures or pseudo seizures, and second, what is causing the real or pseudo seizures. It is possible that these are pseudo seizures. The cause of such pseudo seizures may well be malingering, that is, the patient faking the symptoms or lying about having them. Alternatively, he may be suffering from a conversion reaction, which is the manifestation of a psychiatric illness.

The bottom line here is that this patient likely has a preexisting tendency towards epilepsy that did not develop into an actual seizure disorder. The EEG abnormalities are just markers of this, with no real clinical significance. Some forms of childhood epilepsy are rather subtle in their manifestations. The symptoms may come and go. The progression, severity, and functional impact are just the luck of the draw.

There is a direct relation between the likelihood of a brain injury and the time that a patient is unconscious. The longer the patient is unconscious, the higher the risk of seizure disorders. There is no solid evidence that this patient was unconscious for any length of time in the accident of October 2, YR-2. This mitigates against the existence of a brain injury here.

While I cannot absolutely rule out that the patient had a preexisting seizure disorder exacerbated by this injury, there is no convincing medical proof this has occurred. This patient's inability to provide reliable historical detail makes any comparison of his brain function before and after the fall speculative at best, a garbage-in, garbage-out diagnosis. Therefore, further clinical studies of this patient are not indicated. It is likely that the abnormal EEG readings both are preexisting and dormant.

While I do not disagree with the actual figures Dr. Moretti gave in her deposition for the cost of medical monitoring, these are not causally related to the industrial injury. In my opinion, this patient does not require any future medical services as a result of the fall at Marine Resources. This event has not caused any permanent reduction in his ability to earn a living. He should be able to perform any and all tasks of which he was capable prior to this injury. I would only support an award of medical expenses for the costs of the one-time neurological assessment and EEG following the industrial accident, nothing more.

Thank you for the opportunity to participate in this interesting case.

Very truly yours,

J. Marlene Coffin

J. MARLENE COFFIN, MD

JMC

J. MARLENE COFFIN, MD
BACKGROUND INFORMATION

I graduated from Northwestern University in YR-35. I then went to medical school at Johns Hopkins University and graduated in YR-30. I did my internship and residency at University of Washington Hospital in Seattle in neurological surgery and was the director of the epilepsy center there. I am licensed as a physician and surgeon in the State of Nita, and am a member of the American Board of Neurological Surgery and several other neurological societies.

I do not testify on a regular basis in litigation, other than those involving my own patients. I have testified no more than fifteen times over the course of my career. I will do an occasional forensic medical examination when there is a question about the presence or absence of seizure disorders.

LEARNED TREATISE: DIAGNOSING CLOSED HEAD INJURIES

By Wilbert Von Bulow, PhD

There are two major classes of head injuries: open, where both the skull and brain are damaged, and closed, where the brain is damaged, but the skull is not. Of the two types, closed head injuries are far more common. They can destroy groups of cells within the brain and disrupt nerve pathways and the integration of different brain processes. The effects are complex and subtle. Mental changes dominate over physical ones. Cognitive and emotional handicaps from closed head injuries can lead to long-term disability.

The potential effects of a head injury can be placed in three basic areas of impairment:

1.   Physical impairment, such as lack of coordination, loss of sensory functions, paralysis, seizures, or headaches;

2.   Cognitive impairments affecting memory, attention, concentration, language, and planning and organizing;

3.   Psychosocial problems such as irritability, depression, anxiety, and job-related problems.

Cognitive problems from a head injury can be persistent and chronic, potentially changing the mental capabilities of the patient. The ability to assimilate and process information can be impaired by a closed head injury. Memory defects from whatever cause are difficult to treat.

The usual diagnosis of a head injury case involves the following components:

1.   History of head injury and subsequent mental status since the accident.

2.   General physical examination.

3.   Neurologic examination.

4.   Radiology studies, including CT scan, MRI, and EEG.

The problems from head trauma most often missed by medical and psychological examiners fall into the following categories:

1.   Attentional deficits (e.g., auditory span, fatigue).

2.   Subtle memory disorders (e.g., retrieval of old information).

3.   Executive dysfunctions (e.g., reduced initiative, problems in planning, poor judgment, reduced self-monitoring).

4.   Subtle sensory defects.

There are now hundreds of sophisticated neuropsychological tests that are available for assessing the cognitive function of a patient who has sustained a head injury. However, there are limitations with neuropsychological tests, which may not provide the baseline information needed to precisely estimate the amount of deficit that follows an injury. For example, in most cases of head trauma, there is not objective baseline data from prior to the accident with which to compare post-injury test results.

Seasoned clinical judgment is critical in diagnosing a head injury. The clinician must attempt to make a reasonable estimate of how well the individual functioned prior to the injury. This is not easy to do. It involves looking at the individual's prior performance in school, on-the-job, and in personal relationships. The pre-accident characteristics of each patient must be reconstructed and documented in intricate detail. It is only through this procedure that the clinician may determine whether or not there has been any deterioration from pre-accident function. The claims process always brings up the question of secondary gain—that is, is the patient pretending to have greater difficulty because of the prospect of compensation from a lawsuit? These are things that the clinician must weigh and rule in or rule out.

NITA GENERAL JURY INSTRUCTIONS

The following jury instructions are intended for use regardless of whether the trial is in Nita state court or in federal court. In addition, this file contains special instructions dealing with the law applicable in the particular case. The instructions set forth here state general principles and may be used at the discretion of the trial judge.*

Part I
Preliminary Instructions
Given Prior to the Evidence

Nita Instruction 01:01—Introduction

You have been selected as jurors and have taken an oath to well and truly try this cause. This trial will last one day.

During the progress of the trial there will be periods of time when the Court recesses. During those periods of time, you must not talk about this case among yourselves or with anyone else.

During the trial, do not talk to any of the parties, their lawyers, or any of the witnesses.

If any attempt is made by anyone to talk to you concerning the matters here under consideration, you should immediately report that fact to the Court.

You should keep an open mind. You should not form or express an opinion during the trial and should reach no conclusion in this case until you have heard all of the evidence, the arguments of counsel, and the final instructions as to the law that will be given to you by the Court.

Nita Instruction 01:02—Conduct of the Trial

First, the attorneys will have an opportunity to make opening statements. These statements are not evidence and should be considered only as a preview of what the attorneys expect the evidence will be.

Following the opening statements, witnesses will be called to testify. They will be placed under oath and questioned by the attorneys. Documents and other tangible exhibits may also be received as evidence. If an exhibit is given to you to examine, you should examine it carefully, individually, and without any comment.

It is counsel's right and duty to object when testimony or other evidence is being offered that he or she believes is not admissible.

When the Court sustains an objection to a question, the jurors must disregard the question and the answer, if one has been given, and draw no inference from the question or answer or speculate as to what the witness would have said if permitted to answer. Jurors must also disregard evidence stricken from the record.

When the Court sustains an objection to any evidence the jurors must regard that evidence.

When the Court overrules an objection to any evidence, the jurors must not give that evidence any more weight than if the objection had not been made.

When the evidence is completed, the attorneys will make final statements. These final statements are not evidence, but are given to assist you in evaluating the evidence. The attorneys are also permitted to argue in an attempt to persuade you to a particular verdict. You may accept or reject those arguments as you see fit.

Finally, just before you retire to consider your verdict, I will give you further instructions on the law that applies to this case.

Part II
Final Instructions
General Principles

Nita Instruction 2:01—Introduction

Members of the jury, the evidence and arguments in this case have been completed, and I will now instruct you as to the law.

The law applicable to this case is stated in these instructions and it is your duty to follow all of them. You must not single out certain instructions and disregard others.

Nita Instruction 2:02—Expert Witnesses

You have heard evidence in this case from witnesses who testified as experts. The law allows experts to express an opinion on subjects involving their special knowledge, training and skill, experience, or research. While their opinions are allowed to be given, it is entirely within the province of the jury to determine what weight shall be given to their testimony. Jurors are not bound by the testimony of experts; their testimony is to be weighed as that of any other witness.

Nita Instruction 2:03—Direct and Circumstantial Evidence

The law recognizes two kinds of evidence: direct and circumstantial. Direct evidence proves a fact directly; that is, the evidence by itself, if true, establishes the fact. Circumstantial evidence is the proof of facts or circumstances that give rise to a reasonable inference of other facts; that is, circumstantial evidence proves a fact indirectly in that it follows from other facts or circumstances according to common experience and observations in life. An eyewitness is a common example of direct evidence, while human footprints are circumstantial evidence that a person was present.

The law makes no distinction between direct and circumstantial evidence as to the degree or amount of proof required, and each should be considered according to whatever weight or value it may have. All of the evidence should be considered and evaluated by you in arriving at your verdict.

Nita Instruction 2:04—Concluding Instruction

The Court did not in any way and does not by these instructions give or intimate any opinions as to what has or has not been proven in the case, or as to what are or are not the facts of the case.

No one of these instructions states all of the law applicable, but all of them must be taken, read, and considered together as they are connected with and related to each other as a whole.

You must not be concerned with the wisdom of any rule of law. Regardless of any opinions you may have as to what the law ought to be, it would be a violation of your sworn duty to base a verdict upon any other view of the law than that given in the instructions of the court.

General Instructions for Civil Cases

Nita Instruction 3:01—Burden of Proof; Preponderance of the Evidence

When I say that a party has the burden of proof on any issue, or use the expression "if you find," or "if you decide," "by a preponderance of the evidence," I mean that you must be persuaded from a consideration of all the evidence in the case that the issue in question is more probably true than not true.

Any findings of fact you make must be based on probabilities, not possibilities. They may not be based on surmise, speculation, or conjecture.

Nita Instruction 3:02—Corporate Party

Some of the parties in this case are corporations, and they are entitled to the same fair treatment as an individual would be entitled to under like circumstances, and you should decide the case with the same impartiality you would use in deciding a case between individuals.

Specific Instructions for This Case

Nita Instruction 4:01—Claims of THE PLAINTIFF

The plaintiff, Raymond Garcia, claims that the defendant, Vertex Manufacturing Company, was negligent in two respects, and that Vertex's negligence proximately caused his injuries.

DESIGN DEFECT: First, plaintiff claims Vertex violated its duty to design a product that is reasonably safe and that this proximately caused his injuries. Specifically, plaintiff alleges that the Vertex lift's anti-tipping safety systems' circuit boards were not reasonably safe in their design. Vertex denies this claim.

A product is not reasonably safe as designed if:

1. As designed, the likelihood that the product would cause serious injury similar to that claimed by the plaintiff outweighed the burden on the manufacturer to design a product that would have prevented such injuries; or

2. The product, as designed, was unsafe beyond the reasonable expectations of an ordinary user, considering the reasonable uses of the product, as well as the nature and potential seriousness of the claimed danger.

FAILURE TO WARN: Second, plaintiff also claims Vertex violated its duty to supply the users of its product with adequate warnings or instructions by not issuing a warning about the possible failure of the lift's anti-tipping safety systems. Plaintiff alleges this failure proximately caused his injuries. Vertex denies this claim also.

1. A manufacturer is under a continuing duty to exercise reasonable care to inform users of its products of an unexpected danger arising from a foreseeable use of the product when the manufacturer either has learned of or reasonably should have learned of the danger.

2. In determining whether a product was not reasonably safe, you shall consider the reasonable expectations of an ordinary user of the product, as well as the nature and potential seriousness of the claimed danger.

On each of these two claims, the plaintiff has the burden of proving by a preponderance of the evidence, as defined earlier, each of the following propositions:

1. First, the defendant Vertex acted, or failed to act, in one of the ways claimed by the plaintiff, and

2. Second, in so acting, or failing to act, the defendant Vertex was negligent, and

3. Third, the negligence of the defendant Vertex was a proximate cause of injury to the plaintiff, as I will define that term in these instructions.

Nita Instruction 4:02—Claims of THE DEFENDANT

In addition to denying the plaintiff's negligence claims against it, the defendant, Vertex Manufacturing Company, claims that the plaintiff Raymond Garcia was either the sole or contributing proximate cause of his injuries as a result of his contributory negligence in operating the lift and by failing to check the safety systems before he began his work shift.

Vertex also denies the nature and extent of plaintiff's claimed injuries.

On the defendant's claim of contributory negligence against the plaintiff, Vertex has the burden of proving by a preponderance of the evidence, as defined in these instructions,

1. First, that the plaintiff, Raymond Garcia, acted or failed to act in one of the ways claimed by Vertex, and

2. Second, that in so acting or failing to act, the plaintiff was negligent, and

3. Third, that the negligence of the plaintiff was a proximate cause of his injuries.

The defendant, Vertex, also claims that an entity that is not a named party to this lawsuit, that is, plaintiff's employer, Marine Resources Shipyard, is either the sole or a contributing proximate cause of plaintiff's injuries, failing to adequately train its employees to follow the manufacturer's instructions and inspect the lift before each use.

On the defendant's claims of contributory negligence against Marine Resources, Vertex has the burden of proving by a preponderance of the evidence, as defined in these instructions,

1. First, that the Marine Resources acted, or failed to act, in one of the ways claimed by Vertex, and

2. Second, that in so acting or failing to act, Marine Resources was negligent, and

3. Third, that the negligence of Marine Resources was a proximate cause of the plaintiff's injuries

The plaintiff and Marine Resources have denied that they were negligent and the proximate cause of the plaintiff's injuries.

Nita Instruction 4:03—Negligence

Negligence is the failure to exercise ordinary care. It is the doing of some act that a reasonably careful person would not do under the same or similar circumstances or the failure to do something that a reasonably careful person would have done under the same or similar circumstances.

Ordinary care means the care a reasonably careful person would exercise under the same or similar circumstances.

Nita Instruction 4:04—Contributory Negligence

Contributory negligence is negligence on the part of the plaintiff that is a proximate cause of the injury complained of. If you find contributory negligence, you must determine the degree of negligence, expressed as a percentage, attributable to the plaintiff. The court will furnish you a special verdict form for this purpose. Your answers to the questions in the special verdict form will furnish the basis by which the court will reduce the amount of any damages you find to have been sustained by the plaintiff, by the percentage of such contributory negligence.

Nita Instruction 4:05—Proximate Cause

There may be more than one proximate cause of the same alleged injury. If you find that any entity was negligent and that such negligence was a proximate cause of injury or damage to the plaintiff, it is not a defense that some other cause may have been a proximate cause.

However, if you find the sole proximate cause of injury or damage to the plaintiff was some other cause, then your verdict should be for the defendant.

In the Circuit Court of
Darrow County, Nita
Civil Division

RAYMOND GARCIA,   )

)   Civil Action

      Plaintiff,   )   CA 1948-IL

)

        v.   )   Special Verdict Form

)

VERTEX MANUFACTURING COMPANY   )

)

      Defendant.   )

)

We, the jury, make the following answers to the questions submitted by the Court:

QUESTION NO. 1: Was the defendant Vertex Manufacturing negligent? Answer "Yes" or "No."

ANSWER: Yes _____ No _____

If you answer Question No. 1 "No," sign and return this verdict. If you answer Question No. 1 "Yes," then answer Question No. 2.

QUESTION NO. 2: Was the defendant Vertex Manufacturing's negligence a proximate cause of injury to the plaintiff?

ANSWER: Yes _____ No _____

If you answer Question No. 2 "No" as to the defendant, sign and return this verdict. If you answer Question No. 2 "Yes," then answer Question No. 3.

QUESTION NO. 3: What do you find to be the amount of money that will compensate the plaintiff for his injuries?

$_____

If you answer Question No. 3 with any amount of money, answer Question No. 4. If you find no damages, sign and return this verdict.

QUESTION NO. 4: Was plaintiff, Raymond Garcia, also negligent?

ANSWER: Yes _____ No _____

If you answer Question No. 4 "No," skip Question No. 5 and answer Question No. 6. If you answer Question No. 4 "Yes," answer Question No. 5.

QUESTION NO. 5: Was plaintiff's negligence a proximate cause of the injury to the plaintiff?

ANSWER: Yes _____ No _____

Regardless of whether you answer Question No. 5 "No" or "Yes," answer Question No. 6.

QUESTION NO. 6: Was the nonparty Marine Resources Shipyard also negligent?

ANSWER: Yes _____ No _____

If you answer Question No. 6 "No," skip Question No. 7 and answer Question No. 8. If you answer Question No. 6 "Yes," answer Question No. 7.

QUESTION NO. 7: Was the negligence of Marine Resources Shipyard a proximate cause of the injury to the plaintiff?

ANSWER: Yes _____ No _____

Regardless of how you answer Question No. 7, answer Question No. 8.

QUESTION NO. 8: Assume that 100 percent represents the total combined negligence that proximately caused the plaintiff's injury. What percentage of this combined negligence is attributable to the plaintiff's negligence, the defendant Vertex Manufacturing's negligence, and nonparty Marine Resources' negligence, if any? (Your total must equal 100 percent. If you find the plaintiff or Marine Resources either not negligent or not a proximate cause of the plaintiff's injuries, you must put "0%" next to their name below.)

PERCENTAGE

Plaintiff Raymond Garcia _____

Defendant Vertex Manufacturing Co. _____

Nonparty Marine Resources _____

TOTAL 100%

Sign and return this verdict.

DATE: _____ _____

PRESIDING JUROR

In the Circuit Court of
Darrow County, Nita
Civil Division

RAYMOND GARCIA,   )
)   Civil Action
       Plaintiff,   )   CA 1948-IL
)
         v.   )   Alternate Special
)   Verdict Form on
VERTEX MANUFACTURING COMPANY)   Liability Only
)
       Defendant.   )
)

We, the jury, make the following answers to the questions submitted by the Court:

QUESTION NO. 1: Was the defendant Vertex Manufacturing negligent? Answer "Yes" or "No."

ANSWER: Yes _____ No _____

If you answer Question No. 1 "No," sign and return this verdict. If you answer Question No. 1 "Yes," then answer Question No. 2.

QUESTION NO. 2: Was the defendant Vertex Manufacturing's negligence a proximate cause of injury to the plaintiff?

ANSWER: Yes _____ No _____

If you answer Question No. 2 "No," sign and return this verdict. If you answer Question No. 2 "Yes," then answer Question No. 3.

QUESTION NO. 3: Was plaintiff, Raymond Garcia, also negligent?

ANSWER: Yes _____ No _____

If you answer Question No. 3 "No," skip Question No. 4 and answer Question No. 5. If you answer Question No. 3 "Yes," answer Question No. 4.

QUESTION NO. 4: Was plaintiff's negligence a proximate cause of the injury to the plaintiff?

ANSWER: Yes _____ No _____

Regardless of whether you answer Question No. 4 "No" or "Yes," answer Question No. 5.

QUESTION NO. 5: Was the nonparty Marine Resources Shipyard also negligent?

ANSWER: Yes _____ No _____

If you answer Question No. 5 "No," skip Question No. 6 and answer Question No. 7. If you answer Question No. 5 "Yes," answer Question No. 6.

QUESTION NO. 6: Was the negligence of Marine Resources Shipyard a proximate cause of the injury to the plaintiff.

ANSWER: Yes _____ No _____

Regardless of how you answer Question No. 6, answer Question No. 7.

QUESTION NO. 7: Assume that 100 percent represents the total combined negligence which proximately caused the plaintiff's injury. What percentage of this combined negligence is attributable to the plaintiff's negligence, the defendant Vertex Manufacturing's negligence, and nonparty Marine Resources' negligence, if any? (Your total must equal 100 percent. If you found the plaintiff or Marine Resources either not negligent or not a proximate cause of the plaintiff's injuries, you must put "0%" next to their name below.)

	PERCENTAGE
Plaintiff Raymond Garcia	_____
Defendant Vertex Manufacturing Co.	_____
Nonparty Marine Resources Shipyard	_____
TOTAL	100%

Sign and return this verdict.

DATE: _____   _____

PRESIDING JUROR

The NITA Foundation

supports NITA's core values of excellence, ethics, mentoring, inclusiveness, justice, and philanthropy through our various programs. We strive to give back to our global community by supporting the work of attorneys engaged in the representation of the underserved, indigent, and disenfranchised. To learn more about NITA's publications, programs, or the work of our Foundation, please visit us online at www.nitafoundation.org or by calling (877) 648-2632.

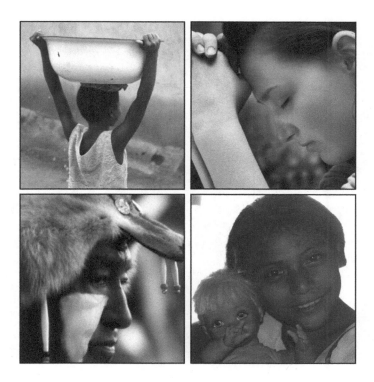

The NITA Foundation